Horace Nutter Colbath

The Barnstead reunion, celebrated at Barnstead,

N.H., August 30, 1882

Horace Nutter Colbath

The Barnstead reunion, celebrated at Barnstead,
N.H., August 30, 1882

ISBN/EAN: 9783337732202

Printed in Europe, USA, Canada, Australia, Japan

Cover: Foto ©ninafisch / pixelio.de

More available books at **www.hansebooks.com**

THE

BARNSTEAD REUNION,

CELEBRATED AT

BARNSTEAD, N. H.

AUGUST 30, 1882,

EDITED BY

HORACE N. COLBATH.

CONCORD, N. H.:
PRINTED BY IRA C. EVANS.
1884.

CONTENTS.

Vote of Publication,	2
Editor Appointed,	2
Introduction,	5
Officers of the Association,	7
Executive Committee,	8
Town Committee,	8
Auxiliary Committee,	8
Other Committees,	9
Programme,	12
List of Sentiments,	13
Address of Welcome, by C. S. George,	15
Poem, by Laura G. Carr,	22
The Dinner,	26
Poem, by H. C. Canney,	26
Letter from S. D. Jewett,	28
" " J. C. Scriggins,	30
" " William G. Drew,	32
Address by H. A. Tuttle,	32
" " E. S. Nutter,	34
" " M. B. V. Edgerly,	36
" " C. M. Murphy,	37
" " J. P. Newell,	38
" " F. H. Lyford,	41
" " J. D. Nutter,	43
" " J. H. Kent,	46
Letter from J. S. Hoitt,	49

Letter from T. E. Barker, . . 50
" " H. H. Huse, ... 50
Hymn, by Mrs. Darius Frink, . . . 52
Address by H. A. Dodge, . . 53
" " J. G. Sinclair, . . 54
Letter of J. B. Garland, . . . 57
Biographical Sketch of Enos George, 60
" " " H. A. Tuttle, . 63
" " " E. S. Nutter, 66
" " " J. G. Sinclair, . 68
" " " M. V. B. Edgerly, 71
" " " C. M. Murphy, 74
" " " Lewis Clark, 78
" " " J. P. Newell, 80
" " " J. H. Kent, . . 82
" " " J. R. Hayes, 87
" " " H. C. Canney, . 89
" ", " George W. Emerson, 92
" " " Geo. S. Pendergast, 95
" " " Harriet P. Dame, 97
" " " Nancy Pendergast, 101
" " " J. D. Nutter, . 104
Contributions, ... 106
Appendix, ... 107

INTRODUCTION.

BARNSTEAD, New Hampshire, situated in the southwestern part of Belknap county, northeast from Concord twenty miles, and bordering on the counties of Merrimack and Strafford, contains thirty-six square miles of territory. Was chartered by Gov. Wentworth May 20, 1727. Containing, in 1880, 1,317 inhabitants.

On the east lie the Blue Hills, on the north are the Alton and Gilmanton mountains, and on the south lies the Catamount, looking down on the valley of the Suncook river as it passes the westerly boundary of the town. It is a region of hill and valley, of beautiful rivers and ponds, and laughing brooks.

A community born and educated amid such scenery, breathing the air of its hills and drinking the waters that flow in hundreds of rills down its hillsides, till they form the Suncook,—must love their childhood home. For the past fifty years Barnstead has been sending out her sons and daughters to other parts of the land to find new homes. Its first emigrants found homes in Massachusetts, Vermont, and New York, and afterwards they sought Ohio, Illinois, Michigan, and Wisconsin. As new territory was opened, they helped swell the mighty stream of emigration that has peopled the great West.

To-day they may be found in twenty-eight states and territories. Some of its sons and daughters are looking out on the Pacific, others are in the valley of the Father of Waters or are fanned by the soft winds of the Gulf.

Scattered over the land, these emigrants have ever yearned for the home of their fathers, while those who remained around the old hearthstones were eager to once more clasp the hands of loved ones, look once more into long remembered faces, and hear once again the voices that were music to their youthful ears.

This was especially true of those who had passed the meridian and were nearing the sunset of life.

By a sort of common consent, residents and emigrants seemed ready for a Reunion of the children of old Barnstead.

The question has been asked, Where did the idea of this reunion originate? This may be a fitting place for answering that question. During the winter of 1877-78, a few of the sons and daughters of Barnstead residing in Concord, N. H., prominent among whom were Col. E. S. Nutter, J. L. Pickering, Esq., George W. Drew, Esq., Mrs. James R. Hill, and Laura Garland Carr, determined to hold a reunion of the sons and daughters of Barnstead living in Concord, with invited guests from the mother town and other places in New Hampshire where Barnstead sons had located.

Such a reunion was held on the evening of February 28, 1878, at the Phenix Hotel, in Concord. There were present from Barnstead, a delegation of sixty citizens, led by the Barnstead Brass Band.

Col. E. S. Nutter presided and made the reception address. Laura Garland Carr read an original poem. Short addresses were made by J. G. Sinclair, Lewis W. Clark, J. Horace Kent, J. P. Newell, and Charles S. George. This, with a supper such as that famous hotel can provide, made the occasion a most enjoyable one.

The resident sons of Barnstead returned home feeling that some day the wanderers from the old town should be invited home to the old domain, and here, amid the scenes of childhood, hold a grand family reunion.

The subject was talked of from time to time, but, from various causes, no decided action was taken until, at the annual town meeting in March, 1882, it was voted to hold a reunion the coming autumn.

Subsequently the following officers were chosen:

PRESIDENT.

Charles S. George.

VICE-PRESIDENTS.

John Walker,
John Pendergast,
Joseph Jenkins,
Caleb Willey,
John B. Garland,
John L. Nutter,
Seth Shackford,

RECORDING SECRETARY.
John H. Jenkins.

CORRESPONDING SECRETARY.
Horace N. Colbath.

TREASURER.
John Franklin Garland.

EXECUTIVE COMMITTEE.
John Waldo,
Thomas L. Hoitt,
Ira L. Berry,
Horatio G. Willey,
Horace Walker.

TOWN COMMITTEE.
George A. Hall,
Albion P. Nutter,
Thomas K. Proctor,
Smith W. Locke,
Seth Shackford,
E. Frank Jones.
Lewis Clark,
Albert F. Shackford,
Charles F. Emerson,
Daniel E. Tuttle,
Hiram Rand,
Frank S. Jenkins,
John Pendergast,
Jacob W. Evans.

AUXILIARY COMMITTEE.
E. S. Nutter, Concord, N. H.;
J. L. Pickering, Concord, N. H.;
H. A. Tuttle, Pittsfield, N. H.;
J. P. Newell, Manchester, N. H.;
C. M. Murphy, Dover, N. H.;

J. Horace Kent, Portsmouth, N. H. ;
George S. Pendergast, Boston, Mass. ;
Jos. R. Hayes, Lowell, Mass. ;
Geo. F. Knowles, Lynn, Mass.

CHAPLAIN.

Rev. William O. Carr.

MARSHAL.

Timothy Emerson.

ASSISTANT MARSHALS.

Frank O. George,
Henry O. Huntress,
John Rand.

SUPERINTENDENT OF HALLS, TENTS, AND GROUNDS.

Dr. George W. Emerson.

COMMITTEE TO PREPARE SENTIMENTS.

Horace N. Colbath.
Charles S. George.

COMMITTEE TO ARRANGE PROGRAMME.

Dr. George W. Emerson,
Horace N. Colbath,
Frank S. Jenkins,
Thomas L. Hoitt.

COMMITTEE ON MUSIC.

Charles E. Walker,
Thomas L. Hoitt.

COMMISSARY.

Frank 'S. Jenkins.

QUARTERMASTER.

John Waldo.

TOAST-MASTER.

Rev. John George.

Thus organized, the work of preparation began. Meetings of committees and sub-committees followed in rapid succession, until a week before the day of reunion, when officers, committees and citizens, uniting, made it their special business.

The arrangements as finally made were as follows:

The Reunion to be held on Wednesday, August 30, 1882, at 10 o'clock A. M.

The President to make the Welcoming Address.

Rev. A. H. Quint, D. D., to deliver an Oration.

Laura Garland Carr to read a Poem.

Dinner, free to all, in the Tent.

Speeches, Sentiments, and Responses at the Stand.

Music through the day by the Barnstead Brass Band. The oldest band in the United States; organized Feb. 22, 1837.

A tent, 78 x 160 feet, was placed on the grounds of Seth Shackford, Esq., adjoining the Town Hall and Congregational Church, and both these buildings were opened to the public. The Speaker's Stand was placed between the Hall and Church; fronting it was the Band Stand.

Under the direction of the Superintendent, Dr. Emerson, the tent was beautifully decorated with flags, bunting, etc., and tables were arranged in the tent to seat 1,050 persons at one sitting.

Such were the measures adopted to welcome home those whose hearts had been throbbing at the thoughts of the reunion.

In every part of the town little plans had been laid to bring families and friends together. It was to be the gathering of a great family.

The number in attendance was estimated to be five thousand, over half that number having partaken of the dinner.

The best order prevailed. It was a meeting of well-dressed, orderly, and respectable men and women, whom any town might be proud to own as her children.

Owing to the prevailing heat and dust, some things were omitted in the reception, and others might have been changed for the better. Yet on the whole, we can say, what every visitor did say, "well done, old Barnstead."

We will now conduct the reader through the various services of the occasion. *The Reunion itself cannot be written or described.*

PROGRAMME.

BARNSTEAD REUNION, AUGUST 30, 1882.

At 10 o'clock A. M.—Meeting of emigrant sons and daughters, former residents, and present residents, on the grounds.

Music by the Barnstead Brass Band.

At 11 o'clock A. M.—Exercises to commence at the Stand:

1st. The Chairman of the Executive Committee to call the assemblage to order, state the order of exercises, and introduce the President of the day.

2d. Prayer by the Chaplain.

3d. Music by the Band.

4th. Address of Welcome by the President.

5th. Oration.

6th. Poem.

7th. Dinner, at 2 o'clock P. M., in the Tent.

8th. Sentiments, Responses, and Reading Letters at the Stand.

List of Sentiments.

1. Old Barnstead—A good town to go from—a better one to return to.

2. A kind remembrance to the sons and daughters of old Barnstead providentially detained from our Reunion.

3. Old Barnstead—Her fair fame a sure passport for her sons wherever they go, her principles a guarantee of success.

4. The adopted sons of Barnstead—They have honored her name, and she rejoices in their success.

5. The emigrant sons and daughters of Barnstead—Wherever may be their abiding place, or whatever their duties, let them never forget that they cannot be delinquent without being degenerate.

6. The town of Barnstead—She loves her hills and beautiful valleys, but feeling the sentiment and borrowing the language of the Roman mother, she points to her children, and exclaims, "These are my jewels."

7. The annual crop produced in Barnstead—judges, clergymen, physicians, merchants, mechanics and farmers—may the crop increase until

she has enough for home consumption and a large surplus for exportation.

8. The friends and scenes of our childhood.

9. The soldier sons of Barnstead—The fathers in the Revolution, the sons in 1812, the grandsons in the Rebellion—the love of liberty constrained them.

10. The birthplace of our fathers—Portsmouth and Newington—names as familiar as household words to every child of Barnstead—may peace and prosperity be in their borders.

11. The host of men whose lives have been made better and happier by choosing for wives, daughters of old Barnstead.

12. The social history and reminiscences of old Barnstead.

13. The resident sons and daughters of Barnstead—May they preserve unsullied its ancient reputation, keep sacred the memory of the fathers, and be always ready to welcome its wandering children to the old domain.

RECEPTION.

Mr. Waldo, Chairman of the Executive Committee, at 11 o'clock, called the vast concourse of people to order, and announced the President of the day, Charles S. George, Esq.

The President introduced Rev. Wm. O. Carr, the Chaplain, who led in prayer—invoking the blessing of their fathers' God to rest upon the children gathered here in their childhood home, and upon the wanderers whose hearts to-day were yearning and whose faces like Hebrew captives were turning toward the home of their fathers.

The following address, welcoming our sons and daughters will win the hearty applause of every child of Barnstead. Mr. George is the son of Rev. Enos George, the first settled minister of Barnstead, who was in his day an eloquent orator, and we believe the verdict of those who listened to this address was—the mantle of the father has fallen on the son.

Mr. George spoke without notes, substantially as follows:

Ladies and Gentlemen:

It is customary on occasions like this for the President, on assuming the chair, to thank the Committee of Arrangements for the high honor conferred on him. This on my part would seem to be rather premature.

Should I succeed in the performance of my duty, it will then be time to return my thanks to the Committee.

But failing, then shall I wish the mantle had fallen on some other man. I have not accepted this position without some misgivings—a plain farmer as I am—and more especially to-day, as I look upon this vast audience, and reflect for a moment upon the intelligence and criticising ability of those who compose it.

And yet I am somewhat relieved of this embarrassment, when I reflect for a moment that you know and I know and everybody knows that there is one prominent characteristic of the people of Barnstead, that whenever and wherever called upon to perform a duty, whether man or woman, whether in war or peace, they make the effort whether successful or not.

And now, as I am a Barnstead man, from the crown of my head to the sole of my foot, I shall make the effort.

And right here, let me say, you are expecting a speech of welcome, all full of "welcome."

This would be the sheerest nonsense. You know Barnstead—you know her people, hence you *know* you are welcome. Rather, let us talk of this good old town. Let us go back more than a hundred years: let us stand on Blue Hills, there can we see a company of brave, strong pioneers, resting on their weary journey; they are now in sight of the promised land. Thirty-six square miles of wilderness lie before them, encircled on every side by mountains and hills, with its giant pines and oaks towering far above all the rest of the forest.

Magnificent sight! Truly it held out no allurement to the lazy, the indolent, the shiftless; and yet how alluring to the strong, the brave, the energetic. They have come from the sea, from the vicinity of Portsmouth, with all that health and vigor that "old ocean" ever gives the dwellers on her shores.

How well with the eye they measure the distance from their prospective home and old Portsmouth—the journey of a day. They look back once more on Portsmouth, in their minds the loveliest spot on earth, possessing the beauty of which she never could be robbed, as Nature held it in her grasp.

They move on; they enter this wilderness, the foliage of whose trees was so deep and so dark that scarce one ray of light could penetrate, and here they wander from hill to hill, from valley to valley, seeking a spot whereon to build them a home.

Others come, of the same mould of character. The town is surveyed, laid off into lots, but no incorporation until the requirements of the British Crown are complied with—a church must be built and the gospel must be preached. And, by the strength of sinewy arms, logs are reared and locked together, the walls are completed, while bark laid from perline to perline—the roof is finished; the inside probably equally rude.

A committee wait upon the Rev. Dr. Adams, of Newington, N. H., to preach the dedication sermon. On horseback he comes,—dismounts,—enters this church,—then and there this good old man lifts up his voice in the wilderness, and with his audience standing, dedicates this rude church to the Triune God.

And where stood the church? Go with me, if you please, to Clarktown. Let us turn to the left, around Mr. Hanson's store. Now we travel by Levi Clark's— down the hill—cross the river—a few rods farther and stop, look to the right, over the wall, and there amid those scattered boulders stood the first church in Barnstead. Truly, that is hallowed ground! and ere that spot is lost to all recognition, let a monument of lasting granite be erected to tell future generations whereon stood Barnstead's first sacred edifice, within whose walls, rude though they were, the gospel in its purity was preached, while our fathers and our mothers chanted the Songs of David with all the devotion and sincerity of angels. It is said that our ancestors were a peculiar people, and why not? Their lot had been cast in the only New England in the world—in the only New Hampshire, and in the only Barnstead then and to-day in all this broad land.

They were proverbial for their shrewdness. The words, "Fools settled in Barnstead," never escaped the lips of man. Should they ever, methinks his head would drop upon his breast never more to rise in the heaviness of his guilt.

If they did not all possess those literary attainments so essential to the well-being and refinement of society— if they could not correctly classify all the wild flowers of the forest, they did possess a judgment and mathematical ability sufficient to tell how many feet in that old-growth pine or in that "brave old oak."

And to obtain such choice lumber for building material, many no doubt were induced to settle here, and year after year this lumber was taken off and transported to Portsmouth, and to-day constitutes the frame and finish of many an old mansion peculiar to that beautiful city. I never walk the streets of Portsmouth, resting my eye on those ancient mansions, without linking them with the early history of Barnstead and with the hardy yeomanry of a generation long since gone.

I never look upon her shipping without realizing the fact that many a ship of Barnstead oak and pine has floated down her harbor, and with sails all spread, out upon the "wide waste of waters," riding triumphant and buoyant as the swan in its element.

I have intimated that the early settlers were not an educated class of people. This does not imply that no improvement in mental culture followed.

Barnstead has probably sent out and is still sending out more teachers than any other town of the same number of inhabitants in the state. At one time no less than four male teachers were engaged in Portsmouth, from high school down, and to-day, while we furnish Dover a mayor, we furnish the state with one sixth of her associate judges and one fifth of her high sheriffs; while its lawyers and doctors are scattered all over the country, from Maine to Georgia and from New Hampshire to California.

And, to-day, Barnstead is represented in twenty-eight states and territories and two foreign countries; and yet as I look out upon this audience, I am reminded that Barnstead's sons and daughters are not all gone. I see before me sons and daughters of old Barnstead who carry in their veins the blood of old John Adams, the foremost in the forum in the "days that tried men's souls."

I see before me sons and daughters who carry in their veins the blood of old John Stark, the hero of Bennington.

Others I see who carry in their veins the blood of one who with a little company under the guidance of old John Sullivan, one dark night, went silently down the Piscataqua river, broke into the fort held by British soldiers, stole the British magazine, returned with it to Durham, and afterwards sent it to Massachusetts, where it was used upon the heights of Bunker Hill. I venture to say no more daring deed was performed in the Revolutionary war, from its incipient stages to the clearing up of the smoke that hung over the city of Yorktown.

Our ancestors were fond of fun, of anecdotes, and of long drawn stories; of tracing their ancestors way back to France, to Scotland, to Ireland, England and Wales.

How interesting to-day would be those stories—with what eagerness we would listen to those genealogies, so correctly, so truthfully told.

Why! my friends, I would give more to-day for a collection of those old stories and those genealogies than I would for a collection of the choicest literature that ever flowed from the pen of man; but they are well nigh lost and forgotten, and the lips that uttered them are sealed, and sealed forever.

The people of Barnstead were strongly attached to each other—strongly attached to their native soil—and it is this element, transmitted down to the present generation, that has brought you here to-day, my stranger friends. And now let me make a short talk to you, and I am done.

To say we are glad to see you, is but a faint expression of our feelings. To shake you by the hand, to recall the scenes of earlier days, gives us a pleasure that vibrates on every artery and permeates every pore of the body.

To know you have left your homes hundreds, nay, thousands of miles behind, to answer to the summons for this gathering, fills us with profoundest gratitude ; while it binds us together with a tie of ten fold tenacity. You are here from your New England homes, from the far West, from the orange groves of the South, from the British dominions, and from the Spanish realms.

And to you, sir,* and yours, who have left your northern home to be with us to-day, permit me to say, that as a home subject to a crown worn by one of the loveliest women the world has ever produced—for more than forty-five years has she sat upon England's throne without a blemish to mar the purity of her character—sir, for the peace of England and England's dominions, long live Victoria.!

And to you, sir,† and yours, who have crossed the ocean to visit once more the home of earlier days, I will say that we do not forget that it was by the generosity and enterprise of a Ferdinand and Isabella that this great and growing continent was given to the world, well nigh four hundred years ago. Sir, may your adopted country ere long return to its former greatness and power, and her people be tempered with the virtues of Alphonzo and his queen.

---

* John D. Nutter, Montreal, Ca.
† Dr. Albert Warren, Madrid, Spain.

To you, sir, and yours, I extend a double welcome, while I wish you, your wife, and little one, a pleasant and safe return to your adopted Spain.

My friends, some of you went forth into the world in childhood; some in maturer years; but the most of you went forth in that happy period of life when the world looked bright—no clouds intervening between you and prosperity and happiness. It was

" In life's morning march,"

ere the bright, unclouded future had told you the story of its storms and its cares! And for your success many a prayer was whispered by the parents and friends you left behind. That you have been successful wherever you have wandered or in whatever part of the country or the world you have made your home, is the sincere and ardent hope of those whom you meet here today.

And now, proud of my position, I stand here, and in behalf of the people of our good old town, greet you all with a welcome in which there is no dissembling, and with a friendship as pure as ever warmed the human heart. We have letters from absent friends, which the Secretary will read to you. And is this all of the reunion?—your presence and these letters from absent friends? Is there no mysterious connection between the living and the dead? Are those "who have gone on before" unconscious of the transactions of this day? *Must* we believe that they are asleep to all the concerns and cares of the living? Ah! *that* sleep means oblivion! Rather let us believe that back from the moment of our creation, onward through the eternal future, there is not one moment lost, not one single link disconnected or broken, in all that endless chain of the soul's immortality. They are here to-day reaching forth the hand in sympathy and friendship from the shadow that veils them from our view!

2

It is this fact that makes this reunion complete. We are *all* here to-day, either mentally, in person, or in sympathy, from the North and from the South, from the East and from the West, and from—beyond the river!

A POEM.

Written for the Barnstead Reunion, August 30, 1882,

BY LAURA GARLAND CARR.

Read by Miss Sophia George.

[Laura Garland Carr, the daughter of William and Mary Jane (Hall) Garland, was born in Barnstead, June 27, 1835, where her childhood was passed. Her father died in her infancy. Her grandfather, Isaac Garland, was an early settler in Barnstead, and reared a large family of sons and daughters, who in early life were all teachers of the schools in Barnstead and elswhere. He was fond of reading, especially poetry, and sometimes wrote verses. He died in 1867, aged ninety-two years. A son, John B. Garland, Esq., owns and occupies the old homestead, to which Mrs. Carr so feelingly refers in some of her poems. Became the wife of N. G. Carr, Esq., of Concord, N. H., Sept. 27, 1864, where she now resides. Her friends hope some day to see the many poetic gems from her pen gathered together and published in a style befitting their worth.

—EDITOR.]

OLD BARNSTEAD.

We talk of buried cities found beneath Italian skies.
Where homes and streets, hidden for years, from out their ashes rise ;
The pleasant thrills that move us, as their relics gather fast,
Tell of a strong, magnetic link binding us to the past.

We need not cross the ocean, friends, nor wander up nor down—
We, who have come to middle life—to find a buried town.
The world is full of them, to-day ; not quite so famed, we know,
Nor covered by Vesuvian fires, so many years ago.

'Tis but the dust that Father Time lets fall in his swift flight—
A golden dust—yet holding close its visions from our sight :
The playgrounds of our childhood! Oh, the homes of earliest days!
We never more may find them, once we leave their mystic ways.

We visit scenes we call the same, and some old trails we find ;
But there's a marked change over all, that cannot be defined.
It gathers deeper, year by year, till each return gives pain,
And memory alone can give the old haunts back again.

And so there's much of sadness in our gathering to-day ;—
For us who went out gay and young, and come back staid and gray ;—
And, while this modern Barnstead has its own fair claims, in sooth,
Forgive us if we cherish best the old town of our youth.

Old Barnstead! Ah, how vast it was!. It almost filled the world!
Not quite,—for wasn't Tuttle's stage, in all its grandeur, whirled,
Once every week, straight through town and off beyond the hills,
Where Dover lay,—a strip of land, with a few noisy mills ?

That stage! No palace car we've seen was half so rich and gay!
It had red curtains, you could see more than a mile away.
And, when close by Lock's Corner school, at Nutter's store, it paused,
What a wild stir of wonderment in our young breasts it caused !

We turned, and stretched our necks, to peer through windows small
  and high,
To catch each crimson flutter in the dust clouds rolling by.
And then the school droned slowly on, while fat old bumble-bees
Looked in on us with husky boom, then whisked off toward the trees.

We followed them with longing eyes, and thought how cool and dense
The shadows lay upon the grass, beyond the pasture fence ;
And wondered if the worm we saw at recess, on the ledge,
Had finished up his jerky job of inching off its edge,

We heard a chipmunk scold and fret, and knew the very stump
Where he was sitting, tail erect, the frisky, saucy hump!
An August-bug, with long-drawn whir-r, went slowly sailing by,
And happy swallows skimmed and wheeled between us and the sky.

And then our eyes went slowly o'er the objects in the room:
The pile of hemlock, by the door, already for a broom;
The oak-leaf festoons on the wall; the long seats, row by row;
The water-pail, on the front bench, with dusty pools below;

The battered old tin dipper, with its rusty base and brim;—
And here we made a pilgrimage in sudden thirsty whim.
Then o'er the teacher's desk we looked, with eager, searching face,
Hoping, amid the knots and stains, a new scene we might trace.

The rusty old box-stove was gay with fragrant tufts of fern,
And all the rambling funnel, in its every crook and turn,
Was misty with asparagus, where flies in busy glee
Swung up and down, so free and glad, it made us wild to see.

Oh, how the time dragged! Are these months so long as first school days?
They are the darkest points I see, way back there in the haze.
Ah, now, when every passing hour is full to overflow,
The thinking on those taskless times is the best rest we know!

No freed, wild creature from the wood ere sped to its abode
More gladly than we bounded home through that long, winding road,
With dinner-pails that swung and flashed at every joyous turn,
And gleaning lessons all the way that were not hard to learn.

Our father's fifty acre farm! How full of nooks t'was stored!
Oh! it seemed larger than this town, with regions unexplored.
We never saw such bees and birds as joined us at our play,
Nor fields so full of sweet wild flowers. You call them weeds to-day.

No modern mower er'e was seen through those fair fields to pass,
Scaring the merry bobolinks from homes deep in the grass;
Nor one of all the clanking things that these new farms infest
Went clattering across those vales, like demons of unrest.

A slender pathway, like a thread, now hidden, and now seen,
Ran through the line of rustling corn and off across the green,
With mazy curves and wayside charms our young feet to beguile,
Till, at the wall, another path met it beyond the stile.

What pleasant people came and went through those remembered ways!
There was no dearth of uncles, aunts, or cousins, in those days.
And oh, the dear old grand-parents, with hearts so warm and true!
So mindful of each childish want in all our noisy crew!

In that old town all things were bright within its ample lines.
No bugs were on the roses then, no blight upon the vines.
And didn't berries ripen sweet through nine months of the year?
Then, oh, the jolly harvest time, with all its added cheer!

There was no empty houses then, beside the roads to rise,
Mocking us with the ghostliness of their dull, vacant eyes;
Nor were there strange new faces glancing from familiar nooks,
Without a hint of love for us in their cold, curious looks.

There were no grave-yards in that town of which we were aware,
Only a few old, mossy graves that always had been there,
With quaint, dark stones telling us when the sleepers went away.
Not one of these cold marble slabs that chill our hearts to-day.

Barnstead! Her fields are rich and green, her meadows fair to see;
Her pasture lands are dotted o'er with cattle, roving free;
Her forests spread their shadows broad in many a sylvan place;
Her hills trail low against the sky in curving lines of grace.

On her fair ponds the lilies lie in all their wealth of bloom,
While from their banks rings out the clear, wild laughter of the loon;
Her streamlets glide down grassy slopes with merry song and flash;
Her waterfalls leap from her heights with frantic plunge and dash.

And though her sons and daughters roam through all the big, round earth,
A goodly company still fills the home that gave them birth.
And younger ones are coming up to join the thinning band,
While peace and plenty, side by side, make glad the pleasant land.

Then here's cheer for Barnstead town, just as she stands to-day;
And here's one for her girls and boys, who've never strayed away;
Another for the distant ones, who hold her memory dear;
And one more for the wanderers, who've once more gathered here.

But when I speak of that old town that has so long been dead,
I feel like standing silently, with bowed, uncovered head.

NOTE. It is with sincere regret that the Editor reports his inability to procure a copy of the Oration of Dr. Quint for publication. Several letters were written him, requesting a copy, but they failed to elicit any response, and reluctantly the book is sent to the printer without it.   [ED.]

THE DINNER.

On adjourning, at 2 o'clock P. M., from the Stand at which the morning exercises had been held, the company moved to the Dining Tent, where tables were loaded with substantial food and varied delicacies, prepared by Barnstead's fair daughters for the guests to the family gathering.

After dinner a short time was spent in social greetings and renewing old acquaintances and friendships, when the thrilling notes of the Band again called them to the Stand.

The President called them to order and introduced Dr. H. C. Canney, of Manchester, who read the following Poem:

BARNSTEAD.

[Written for and read at the Reunion held at Barnstead, N. H., August 30, 1882.]

BY DR. H. C. CANNEY.

Old Barnstead! grand and noble town,
The fairest gem in a nation's crown,
With thy broad fields, thy hills and waters,
Thy noble sons and peerless daughters.

Thy daughters fair, wherever found,
With memories sweet thy name surround;
Thy absent sons, where'er they roam,
Still think of thee, old town, as home.

No skies so fair have they e'er seen,
No birds so gay, no fields so green,
No other waters e'er so bright,
As sparkled to their youthful sight.

Then life seemed bright as morning's dew,
And earth seemed good and pure and true.
O, that those dreams were dreams of truth,—
Those of our free and buoyant youth.

But 'mid this day of festal gladness
We will remember, not in sadness,
How far from childhood's faith we turned,
As we life's bitter lessons learned.

Again we view each treasured nook,
By rocky height or babbling brook,
And they bring back with magic power,
Remembrance of youth's fleeting hour.

It only seems the other day,
We frolicked there in childhood's play,
And we forget the flight of years,
Life's struggles, triumphs, joys and tears.

As here we meet 'mid scenes of yore,
And friend greets friend with joy once more;
We join the sport, and not in vain,
We dream that we are young again.

Though passing time has left its traces
Upon the old, familiar faces;
And many to-day we miss among
Those dear to us when life was young.

Old Barnstead, 'round our natal shrine,
The strongest tendrils always twine,
'Round early friends and playmates dear,
Now in reunion gathered here.

Then let joy's merry tones ring out,
Ring far and wide in gladsome shout,
Till vale and hill shall give reply
In echoes sounding to the sky !

Long may the old town guard with care
That honored station now its share;
And may its truant children all
Return at each reunion's call,

To pass at least one happy day
With those at home, who wisely stay,
To ever keep thy growing fame,—
With them 'tis safe—thy honored name.

From heaven to earth no bliss descends
More pure than greeting childhood's friends;
And may we hope reunions here
Will mark with joy each passing year.

For they will ever truly be
Like islands green in life's drear sea,
And grown more dear as years shall glide
Adown times ever ebbing tide.

Yet 'mid our joys comes thought of pain,
We may not all meet here again;
For one by one we journey 'lone
Unto the land of the unknown.

But through the years of coming time,
As pilgrims in an eastern clime
Gather at Mecca, their shrine so dear—
So may our children gather here.

When earth and time no more shall be,
I hope and trust, old friends, that we
Shall yet a grand reunion hold
'Yond gates of pearl, in streets of gold.

After the Poem, the Secretary read the following letters:

LETTER OF REV. S. D. JEWETT, OF MIDDLETOWN, CONN.

MIDDLETOWN, CT., Aug. 23, 1882.

REV. WM. O. CARR,—

Dear Sir: I have received the invitation of the Ex. Committee to attend the Reunion at Barnstead Aug. 30.

Your letter of the 17th came with the request that I lead in the opening prayer. Could I be present I would stand in my lot, and do what I might to add to the interest of the occasion. But I must decline to accept your kind invitation. I excuse myself on the score of distance, home duties and age.

The first settlers of Barnstead are well remembered by me. Although I have not lately visited my native place bodily, yet I am often there in spirit. Among the dead and living are my kindred. I can now see distinctly the form and face of Esquire Charles Hodgdon, Leftenant Benjamin Nutter, Uncle Lord, Uncle Joseph and Deborah Bunker, Deacon Ebenezer Nutter and his wife, riding six miles on horseback to meeting.

I have the History of Barnstead and read it with great pleasure, and if it has some irrelevant matter and a superabundance of poetry, it is what was wanted—a correct history of Barnstead. It need not be said that the pioneers of Barnstead were almost a unit in politics. At one time there were but two Federal votes found in the ballot-box— one of these was thrown out by my father, the other by Uncle Locke of the north part of the town. Your venerable predecessor, Rev. Enos George, was earnest and efficient to perpetuate the same ratio.

If Barnstead has not increased in population as some towns have, it is because so many of her sons have emigrated.

I am surprised to see the catalogue of professional and educated men that Barnstead has sent out. What town of equal population can compare with it in this respect? I have many pleasant memories of Barnstead Parade. I am now over eighty years old, and have some of the peevishness of old age; but when I remember the follies and mischief of early days, my fault-finding is suppressed and I am charitable.

God bless old Barnstead! He brought a strong and vigorous colony there, led by a pious servant of his own choice. He has sustained them since, and now permits them to sit in peace and plenty under their own vine and fig tree. This Reunion should be full of gratitude to God, and full of faith in him for the future.

Let it close with every voice in a grand chorus,

"Praise God from whom all blessings flow."

From your aged townsman,

S. D. JEWETT.

LETTER OF J. C SCRIGGINS, ESQ.

Storm Lake, Iowa, Aug 11, 1882.

Horace N. Colbath, Esq.,—

Dear Sir: I received your kind invitation to attend the Reunion of the Sons and Daughters of Barnstead, Aug. 30th.

I should be happy to come and see long remembered faces and take one more look over the hills and valleys of my native town, the home of my boyhood, before I go to that "bourne from which no traveller returns."

But it is impossible. I am all alone, and have cows, horses, and swine to care for and look after as well as farm crops to gather.

I cannot write you my feelings, as I am not used to much writing, but I enclose some verses that I found in a paper, that in many respects truly expresses my own experience:

> In the home of my childhood, where tall poplars grew,
> Was a huge kitchen fire-place homely to view,
> With its old-fashioned crane and its trammels of wire,
> That swung the "cook-pot" o'er the old kitchen fire.
>
> Back-logs were, in winter, piled up to the flue,
> With fore-sticks of hick'ry, or maple in lieu;
> Whence bright cheerful flames would leap higher and higher,
> Till all was aglow 'round the old kitchen fire.

In autumn the bacon and shoulders and hams
Were hung up to cure in those ample old jambs,
And all the home comforts that heart could desire,
Were plenty and free 'round that old kitchen fire.

When the chores were all done, and the back-log in place
We drew round the table, and bowing for "grace,"
All joined in thanksgiving, pronounced by the sire,
For blessings surrounding our old kitchen fire.

Oft-times was that kitchen the neighbors' resort
For social enjoyment or juvenile sport,
And children would cluster around our grandsire
To hear his war-tales by the old kitchen fire.

The purest enjoyments I ever have known
Were those when I mingled at home with my own—
With parents and children, and household entire,
Assembled around the dear old kitchen fire.

One soul was as gentle and sweet as the dove—
The bond of our circle, its centre of love,
Whose hands though oft weary, seem never to tire
Of labors of love 'round the old kitchen fire.

As the mother-bird guardeth the nest of her brood,
Thus watchful was she for our safety and good;
And often she toiled, after all would retire,
Our garments to mend by the old kitchen fire.

In search of enjoyment I've roved the world round,
'Mong the grave and the festive, and yet I've not found
In all life's allurements one charm to admire
Like the home scenes of yore 'round the old kitchen fire.

Thanking you for your kind invitation, I am
        Your ob't servant,
                JOSHUA C. SCRIGGINS.

LETTER OF WILLIAM G. DREW.

QUINCY, PLUMAS CO., CALIFORNIA,
August 13, 1882.

HORACE N. COLBATH,—

Dear Sir: I hereby acknowledge the receipt of your kind invitation to be present at the Barnstead Reunion, with sincere regrets that I cannot be there.

Yet I would say to the sons and daughters of Barnstead, Dear Brothers and Sisters, Greeting from one who holds in most affectionate remembrance the home of his childhood—old Barnstead, in Yankee land.

You may be sure, my friends, I am with you in spirit although materially I am three thousand miles away.

When I first came to California, I was introduced to a gentleman, a native of New Hampshire, who asked from what part of the state I came. With pride I answered from Barnstead. "A good place to come from," said he, emphatically.

But I, for one, think it is a good place to live in, and a good place to return to; and truly I hope when you have another Reunion I may be there in person.

Wishing you all much pleasure at your Reunion,

I am, with respect, yours, &c.,

WM. GARLAND DREW.

1st SENTIMENT:

Old Barnstead—A good town to go from—a better one to return to.

Responded to by Hon. H. A. Tuttle, as follows:

Mr. President, Ladies and Gentlemen:

Thirty years ago to-day I left the old shoe shop, opposite Shackford's Hotel, and went out into the world to seek my fortune.

I went with the kind wishes of the people ringing in my ears, and with the thought that after all Barnstead was a pretty good place from which to go.

Somehow I never could make up my mind to settle in the rich regions of the West as have many emigrants from Barnstead.

I still clung to the old Granite State, and finally adopted the neighboring town of Pittsfield as my home. I went into business there and soon found, by the liberal patronage and cheering words of her people, how Barnstead would stand by her sons.

Yes, ladies and gentlemen, Barnstead is a good town to go from—you are never forgotten. The people rejoice with you in your prosperity, and weep with you in your adversity.

What a hearty welcome they give you when you return ! and how proud you are that Barnstead is your native town.

Barnstead ! The birthplace of such men as the orator of the day, the learned Quint of Dover, Judge Clark of Manchester, the " Barnstead Boy," Hon. John G. Sinclair, Hon. J. P. Newell, Col. Murphy the present Mayor of Dover, Col. Edgerly of Manchester, and a host of others who are present here to-day.

But who have always wished us God-speed in every good purpose ? Who have given us the heartiest welcome to-day ? Who have entertained us pleasantly ? Who have supplied the wants of the inner man ? Without whom would this Reunion have been an utter failure ? The sons of Barnstead ? No ! The *daughters* of Barnstead ! May they live long and prosper.

Sir: We have found out to-day that Barnstead is even a better place to return to, than to go from. Let us return oftener ! Let the old ties of kinship and of friendship be closer drawn about us, and may old Barnstead see our faces oftener in the future than she has in the past.

2d SENTIMENT:

A kind remembrance to the Sons and Daughters of Barnstead providentially detained from our Reunion.

Response by Col. E. S. Nutter, Concord, N. H., as follows:

Mr. President:

It would have pleased me far better had it fallen to the lot of some more eloquent son of our good old town to respond to this toast. Yet I am sure that no one among them all, at home or abroad, cherishes a warmer love for old Barnstead, or a stronger regard for all her sons and daughters, wherever they may be found. There is no more pleasant occurrence in ordinary life than the family reunion, where all the absent sons and daughters come back to the home of their childhood and gather beneath the old roof-tree, as in the days of the past. Ours, to-day, is a reunion upon a larger scale. Many families are gathered here, all with a common interest, all responding to the call of a common mother—the town whose name we honor, and whose soil we love. While we live the memory of this occasion will be one of the brightest things of life. Yet there is no pleasure without alloy; no joy without some tinge of sadness. As we have met old friends and renewed old friendships, we are sensibly reminded of the fact that there are those who were with us in other days, whose faces we have not seen and whose voices we have not heard to-day. Some of them—many, indeed—have passed beyond the reach of any mortal mother's call. Others may have received the summons, but have been unable to respond. Some are disabled by the infirmities of age—worn and wearied by long and faithful services in life's great fields of labor. Others are confined by business cares which cannot be laid aside, even for a brief interval.

Others, still, are separated from us by long distance, beyond their means to overcome, however strong their inclination and desire. There is no section of the state, no part of the country, where the sons and daughters of Barnstead are not to be found; and wherever they are, we may be sure they have done and are doing their duty well and faithfully. In every walk of life—in law and politics, in the ministry and in the school-room, in trade and manufacture, and in every line of industry, the representatives of our good old town are found in the front ranks. Some of the most successful of the number are here to-day.

We rejoice in their presence, and gladly listen to their words of kindly cheer.

But to the absent ones, whether known or unknown to worldly fame and honor, our thoughts turn at this time.

They are our brothers and sisters—children of the dear old mother town—and wherever they are, scattered up and down the state, or all over the Union, or even beyond its borders as many are, we may be sure that their hearts are with us now, even as our hearts go out to them. Though absent in body they are present in spirit. They have not forgotten their native hills and valleys and the friends and associations of childhood and youth. They will cherish the memory of these as long and faithfully as the lessons of honesty, frugality, and patriotism, which they learned in their midst—and have followed through life. Though with us on this glad occasion in thought and wish alone, we cannot doubt that our absent friends await with deepest interest the report of our reunion, and all its exercises and details.

They will hear of it in their homes, they will read the story of its grand success with true and loyal pride; but the half even can never be told or written.

Only those who participated in person can have an realizing sense of the pleasure and success of this day and occasion. So it is that we regret, as deeply as they can do, that so many of our friends have been unable to gather with us to day—that we do not enjoy their presence, and that the full measure of what we do enjoy cannot be shared with them. We can only send them fraternal greeting, and the assurance of affectionate regard.

3d SENTIMENT:

Old Barnstead—Her fair fame a sure passport for her sons wherever they go; her principles a guarantee of success.

Col. M. B. V. Edgerly, of Manchester, N. H., responded, briefly, as follows:

Mr. President, Ladies and Gentlemen:

To-day the sons and daughters of Barnstead meet to celebrate their first reunion.

Let us consider for a moment some of the characteristics of the old town and its children.

There is a natural variety of men and women. Some are brave and intelligent, some timid and despondent; and to understand why all are not equal, why one should be more especially fitted to their work than another, we should go back to their birthplace, to their first surroundings, and find out the peculiar characteristics of their birthplace—for in every country man is deeply rooted into the soil of nature.

Generally the sons and daughters of Barnstead are pushing, energetic, and trustworthy, and are striving to reach an honorable position in life; and when they have reached the pinnacle of their ambition, they bring not only honor to themselves but to their native town, the birthplace where their principles were nurtured and sustained.

The better and higher the principles, the more capable the people, and more richly endowed with honesty and integrity.

Both the mental and physical structure of mankind depend more or less upon surroundings.

The lovelier the landscape the more poetic the race; and in such a town as old Barnstead, undulating with hill and vale, mankind contracts a temperament and a character corresponding to it.

I am inclined to believe that whatever of fame and honor has been achieved by the sons and daughters of Barnstead they owe much to the inspiration born of the rugged hills of their native town. And I am glad to know that she has sent into the various walks of life her sons and daughters who have shed a brilliancy upon her name and exerted a healthful influence upon the affairs of the state, of which we may all be proud.

With many thanks, Mr. President, for your flattering introduction and kind wishes, and with bright hopes for the future prosperity of old Barnstead, allow me to give place to others.

4th SENTIMENT:

The adopted sons of Barnstead—They have honored her name and she rejoices in their success.

Hon. C. M. Murphy of Dover, N. H., responded, as follows:

Mr President:

I have no difficulty in admitting that a well-situated, thrifty, and attractive New England town, must owe a good deal to its adopted sons. One is not consulted about his birthplace, but his head and heart have to do with the choice of associates and surroundings. My recollections of Barnstead are exceedingly pleasant. Many changes have taken place in Yankee land since I was a long-legged boy in this town. Many of the old seaports are now well-nigh deserted; regions that were then wholly agricultural, are now wholly manufacturing; turnpikes then much frequented, are now largely abandoned; capital has changed quarters, and the future promises other and still more important departures. But to me, Barnstead still preserves its old-time certainty and invariability. The vicissitudes which have disturbed other places, seem not to have affected this. If my opinion is a correct one, and I entertain no doubt and fear no contradiction, there must be a good reason for such steadiness, integrity, and singleness of purpose. Shall the reason be sought for in its early history? My friend, Dr. Quint, who lives a part of his time in the 17th century, and knows more about the early settlers of New Hampshire towns than most of us do of our childhood, can answer the question. Picturesque or ugly, we are bound to speak well of our birthplace, but it is a good test of one's liking for a locality, if coming to it as a stranger, and leaving it before maturity, he loves to revisit it, and continues through busy, engrossing years, to hold pleasing and hearty interest in its welfare. This test, Mr. President, I meet fully, and confidently believe, that time, in this respect, can work no change in me.

5th SENTIMENT:

The emigrant sons and daughters of Barnstead —Wherever may be their abiding place or whatever their duties, let them never forget that they cannot be delinquent without being degenerate.

Hon John P. Newell, of Manchester, N. H., eloquently responded as follows:

Mr. President, Ladies and Gentlemen,
Fellow-Citizens of Barnstead:

I am glad to be with you to-day, and to be permitted to look once more into your honest faces and to feel once more the pressure of your friendly hands. I am glad that those of you who still abide in or near your ancestral homes have found it in your hearts to inaugurate and carry into successful execution this reunion of the sons and daughters of old Barnstead. The occasion revives old associations and brings back fondly to my memory the happy days of my boyhood, and all the cherished friendships of my early life.

Though it is now many years since my father moved into an adjoining town, and made a home for himself and his family. Yet even to this day, whenever in my dreams I am in my father's house, it is always the dear old home on the Province road, in South Barnstead, where I was born.

Every rod of my father's farm, and every spot in all the neighborhood, is to me hallowed ground; and I adopt, as expressing my own feelings, the words of the poet:

> "How dear to my heart are the scenes of my childhood,
> As fond recollection presents them to view:
> The orchard, the meadow, the deep tangled wild-wood,
> And every loved spot my infancy knew."

A distinguished son of New Hampshire, who, in his young manhood, joined the tide of emigration towards the setting sun and made himself famous in a western state, is said once to have made the remark that New Hampshire was a good state to emigrate from, and many have supposed that Gen. Cass meant this in disparagement of his native state. But, no; he intended to say, that the training a young man gets in New Hampshire in matters of industry, enterprise, economy, and unwavering honesty, will ensure his success wherever he may go and whoever may be his competitors. And if the sons of Barnstead who have gone forth from your midst have achieved anything of success—and you have no occasion to blush for them to-day—it is because of the training they received in the dear old homes in Barnstead, and of the healthful influences that were about them during all the years of their childhood and youth; and among those influences, whose tendency was to form high and manly character, were the well kept public and select schools in town, and the honest life and worthy example of the fathers and mothers. But not the least among these influences that helped to form the character of the young, was the elevating influence of that good man who was often a teacher in our public schools and who for more than fifty years was a minister of the gospel in this town. I refer, of course, Mr. President, to your honored father, the Rev. Enos George, of blessed memory.

I see by the census reports that the population of Barnstead is less than it was some years ago. In seeking for the causes of this diminished population, I desire to ask, Where now are those homes, that used to exist here, full of healthy and happy children? Why, I remember four families that once lived over on the Province road in which there were fifty-four children, and the number in the several families increased in regular progression—twelve, thirteen, fourteen, and fifteen—fifty-four in all.

I believe in the policy and the justice of giving pensions to those brave but disabled soldiers, who, during the late rebellion, endured hardships and imperiled life in defence of the American Union. But I think, Mr. President, it would be a no less wise and just thing to pension those mothers of a numerous offspring.

Another reason for the depopulation of these country towns may be found in the fact that the boys who have been born and reared here, as soon as they grow to manhood, and even before that time, leave their homes and their fathers' farms, and flock to the cities in quest of employment.

In this way, families are broken up, and the children are scattered far and wide, leaving father and mother in their enfeebled age to plod on, as best they may, until life's journey is finished.

In many cases I believe this to be a grave mistake, if, indeed, it be not a crime. Let the homes, as far as this can be done, be made beautiful and attractive, well supsupplied with choice books and daily or weekly papers and whatever else is calculated to embellish life and form manly character, and then let the boys remain at home, or in near neighborhood of home, a help to each other and be a comfort and solace to their fathers and mothers, to whom they are bound by every tie of nature and by every consideration of gratitude and love.

And now, Mr. President, I will close with a heartfelt wish for continued prosperity and happiness to all the good people of old Barnstead.

6th SENTIMENT:

The town of Barnstead—She loves her hills and beautiful valleys, but feeling the sentiment and borrowing the language of the Roman mother, she points to her children, and exclaims, " These are my jewels."

Rev. Frank H. Lyford was called upon to respond to this sentiment. Having taken the stand, he said:

Mr. President, Ladies and Gentlemen:

Worthy sons and daughters of noble sires : Jewels of old Barnstead : Happy am I to greet you on this occasion : An occasion alike honorable to yourselves and those who have gone before you.

Why! bless your dear souls, it does me good to behold your upturned faces, with blooming cheeks and sparkling eyes.

The very air we breathe is fraught with beauty and fragrance. And, although not to the manor born, yet my associations with this people, and my former residence in this good old town, have been of such a nature as to make every inch of her soil, from Beauty Hill to Blue Job, and all the way along the beautiful Suncook, dear to my heart and memory. And every man, woman, and child among you seems, as it were, my own kith and kin.

One can scarcely enjoy an occasion like this, with the cordial greetings and hearty handshakings of so many dear old friends, without being made a better and happier man.

May we go from this Reunion to our several homes, better prepared to take up the weapons of our warfare in life's great struggle, and, the good Lord helping us, may we each be enabled to accomplish more for His glory and the good of man than hitherto we have done.

I am proud of my connection with this people,—proud of this occasion,—glad of the high privilege of being present with you to-day, and of being counted worthy of holding a position among the former residents of your town, a town whose people have honored me with their confidence and support on more than one occasion.

Although not in the political world at present, there is something in our surroundings, or in the air we breathe to-day, that seems to spur me up to do something entirely out of my line. I see upon this stand some noble specimens of "Young America"—sons of old Barnstead,—representative men of different political organizations, any one of them worthy and well-qualified to fill the chair of state, and had we come home to-day to vote, instead of shaking hands and eating your "Big Dinner," were Col. Edgerly or Col. Tuttle the candidate for Governor, I think I would hardly be restrained from letting out the old war-whoop of "All for Edgerly," or "All for Tuttle."

You, sir, remember the story of the old maid's prayer for a husband, and its final conclusion, "Any body will do." And so with me to-day, any body will do, so he be a son of the good old town of Barnstead.

Wishing you all abundant success and prosperity in this life, and a happy home in the "Sweet Bye and Bye," I leave you with the hope that your young men may be true to the teachings of the fathers, and your young women may imitate the virtues of the mothers, to whom Barnstead may point, and proudly exclaim, "These are my jewels!"

7th SENTIMENT:

The annual crop produced in old Barnstead— Judges, Clergymen, Physicians, Merchants, Mechanics, and Farmers — May the crop increase until she has enough for home consumption and a large surplus for exportation.

Response by John D. Nutter, Esq., of Montreal, Canada, substantially as follows:

Mr. President:

It would be an injustice to you as well as myself, did I not acknowledge the kind words you have spoken and the cordial welcome you have extended to those who have come from a distance to join you in the greetings, pleasures, and festivities of this Reunion.

It is exceedingly pleasant to be remembered by the companions of our boyhood and school days. It adds another link to the chain that binds us to the place of our birth—home! that sweetest word and dearest place in this world.

The multitude of the sons and daughters of Barnstead who are here to-day, from far and near, proves this assertion beyond a doubt.

Here we delight to come, and around the old fireside greet each other, and for a brief time hear and recount to each other the vicissitudes through which we have passed since we left the paternal roof.

I have just visited the place where I was born. How well I remember its surroundings—the woodland, where I hunted the wild partridge—the brook beyond, meandering through the Munsey Meadow, winding its way to the Parade, and then lost in the Suncook; by its side, with hook and line, you and I, Mr. President, have spent many happy hours, patiently waiting for the bite of the tiny trout.

The orchard, where every good tree was known and named, is but a shadow of what it then was, only here and there, like sentinels, are a few trees standing.

The old cottage, with its blazing hearth, the room where we lived, my mother, the centre of the family group (my father having died before I could remember), seated at the table with her knitting, and the children, by the light of a tallow candle, studying the lessons for to-morrow's school.

I saw to-day the place where stood the old school-house, but how changed! then a small square building, painted red, with a pointed roof, the wooden desks covered with jack-knife engravings and the names of its occupants—the high desk by the door—the speaking form, and the old fire place, have long since passed away.

The teacher, Mr. President, was none other than your father, the Rev. Enos George, and my heart prompts me to pay my tribute to his memory and worth. No words of mine can do justice to him as a teacher, pastor or man.

His name and memory is engraved on all our hearts. Barnstead can never forget him. He labored here fifty years with untiring zeal, as a teacher in education and religion, and I believe his influence for good is felt here to-day.

As a minister, clad in that sombre garb, I almost feared him, but at his school I lost that fear.

He was a good teacher, strict in discipline but just,— what he promised he performed. I well remember the story of the unruly pupil, whom Parson George had promised to punish the *next* day, coming to him asking to be punished at once, as he did not want to dread it so long.

More than a generation has passed since I went out from home, an indigent boy, with a limited education, and no knowledge of the world, to try and gather around me the comforts of a home. Time has changed us all—those smiling girls are now staid matrons, those happy, careless boys are now earnest men upon whose brows the snow of winter is fast falling. It has been my lot to have seen something of the world, and I have yet to find a place that I would exchange, as a home, for New England. God bless her. I love her people, her religion, her morality, her system of schools, her equal laws, and strict administration of the same.

I hail the Old Flag that is floating above us. I have seen it in distant lands, and felt proud that I could claim it as my birthright. More than a quarter of a century has passed since I have lived under the jurisdiction of the United States. Circumstances that led me away when a boy have kept me away ever since. Still I claim old Barnstead as my home.

The pleasure of meeting here has its sting. The thought that we are soon to part presses upon me. Sadly I turn away from the scenes I have always loved, leaving buried in your soil my ancestors. They lie here in your sacred keeping. Let them sleep on quietly until that other and last great Reunion. Then, sir, and not till then, shall we all meet again.

8th SENTIMENT:

The friends and scenes of our childhood.

Col. J. Horace Kent had been invited to respond to this sentiment, and had written his acceptance; but at the last moment was detained by imperative business, and was unable to be present at the Reunion, much to his regret, as well as to the regret of his many early friends. Col. Kent, however, sent the following address, delivered at the Barnstead Reunion in Concord, N. H., February 28, 1879, in response to a similar sentiment.

Mr. President and Friends:

This pleasant occasion affords me a double pleasure tonight. First, because it brings me into agreeable associations with my native townsmen and women, many of whom I am personally attached to from lengthy and friendly acquaintance, while others are familiarly known through their honorable reputations for correct principles, as firm and unyielding as the granite hills of our good old state. Secondly, I am pleased and I think benefited by being, if even for only a short time at least, released from the toils and cares of everyday life, and allowed to go back in recollection to our old birthplace and review the dear old scenes of our youth, where peace and plenty, fun and frolic, were the order of the day, and the sweet sleep of innocence the order of the night. There is nothing better, if it be only in fancy, to soften the heart and clear the head, Mr. President, than an occasional visit to the homes of our childhood, to hear once more the old church bell, to see the venerable school-house, and romp and gallop on the old playground. It, sir, is a sort of elixir of life which prolongs our existence; or adds to it at least, by permiting us to again enjoy the sweet delights of our youth. Notwithstanding our native town was and is a small one, its children have been spread over a wide surface of the country, and have been somewhat noted as being pretty enterprising fellows if not over and above smart, and, as I cast my eyes around me, I don't think the present company ought to be excepted. It has produced a representative in congress and a U. S. senator, and another "Barnstead Boy" is very prominently mentioned for senatorial honors should the tide turn in favor of the party of which he is so distinguished and able a representative, and I am glad to see him here to-night. Numerous other citizens have held prominent governmental positions, and among our state officials we find that heretofore she has been honorably and creditably represented, and is, at the present time, furnishing one of its most dignified and trusted judicial officers. I am gratified to see him, my companion of the old brick school-house, here also.

As to our prominent public teachers sent abroad, the gentlemen who have preceded me have justly alluded to them, and, my friends, I think, according to our population, Barnstead can carry off the palm in this respect. Besides those in other places I can call to mind four or five who were at Portsmouth at one time. There were Pickering, Chesley, George, and Tasker, and I don't think I shall ever forget the latter. He was an excellent teacher (and I was one of his pupils at Portsmouth), always opened the morning exercises with prayer, and the prayer invariably ended as follows: "Amen, come down here, Kent," and as invariably I was punished. In after life Tasker told me that I was the best boy to learn my lessons, and deviltry as well, that he had in the school. An allusion has been made by one of the speakers that he believed it would be as well if not better if so many young men did not leave their native homes. I caught his inspiration, and asked myself the question, "How many of us have found a better fortune than we left behind us?"

For my own part, although I have seen much of the world, have dwelt in large cities, and mixed with all classes of people, enjoyed all the pleasures and delights which are to be found in rich and populous places, and been honored with positions beyond my desert, I sometimes feel that when I left old Barnstead I parted with a buoyancy of feeling, a hopefulness of heart, a homely simplicity of spirit that I have never since regained; and I look back with almost envy to the old associations and pleasures of youth, in and around the old homestead, and faintly realize how old father Adam must have felt when he took a farewell look at Paradise as he left it to labor and struggle in the world beyond.

Mr. President, I could mention reminiscences, anecdotes, noble acts, patriotic purposes, and Christian virtues of many of our townsmen and women, several of whom having fulfilled their mission on earth, their spirits have been wafted to heaven. Some of them have already been appropriately alluded to by others; and I know that if left to the ready and eloquent Sinclair to review he will cover all the ground that has been left out or neglected. I cannot further take up your time, and will say in conclusion that I heartily enjoy and appreciate this pleasant reunion of old friends and fellow townsmen, and hope, as has been previously suggested, we may have many more such gatherings to remind us of the times behind us, and nerve us for fresh duties in the days to come.

I have brought with me, to share my enjoyment, my dear old Barnstead mother, my Massachusetts wife, and my California son, and though they never speak in meeting, I am sure that they feel all that I feel, and I feel more than I know how to express. Let me close with the following sentiment:

The natives of Barnstead and their descendants—May Providence multiply their number, substract from their sorrows, divide their cares, add to their comforts, and close up life's accounts with an honest balance on the right side of the ledger.

9th SENTIMENT:

The soldier sons of old Barnstead—The fathers in the Revolution, the sons in 1812, the grandsons in the Rebellion—the love of liberty constrained them.

Responded to by letters from Col. Jas. S. Hoitt, of Laconia, N. H., a native of Barnstead and a veteran of 1812; from Col. Thos. E. Barker, of Boston, Mass., a native of Barnstead and Colonel of the 12th Regiment in the Rebellion; from Hon. Henry H. Huse, of Manchester, a former resident of Barnstead, who served in the 8th Regiment as Captain and Major.

LETTER OF COL. JAMES S. HOITT.

LACONIA, Aug. 15, 1882.

H. N. COLBATH, ESQ.,—

Dear Sir: Your favor of the 12th inst. is at hand.

It would give me great pleasure to be present at the Reunion Aug 30th, and respond to the best of my ability to the sentiment, " The soldier sons of Barnstead."

It was my privilege to meet some of its sons in 1812— who went forth with me to defend our country's honor.

I was personally acquainted with many of the Revolutionary fathers of old Barnstead, and knew their sturdy patriotism.

In the late Rebellion, we know Barnstead was not found wanting; her sons nobly responded to the call for volunteers, and many of them sealed their devotion with their lives.

I am now over four score years old, but if my health continues as good as at present, I will try and be present.

Always entertaining great respect for " Old Barnstead " and its inhabitants, I remain

Yours truly,

JAMES S. HOITT.

LETTER OF THOMAS E. BARKER.

BOSTON, Aug. 15, 1882.

HORACE N. COLBATH, ESQ.,—

Dear Sir: On my return this afternoon after an absence of several days, I received yours of the 12th, asking me to respond to the sentiment "The soldier sons of old Barnstead," at the Reunion Aug. 30. It would afford me great pleasure to be present at the Reunion, and if there to say a word—though I could do the subject feeble justice.

A sentiment so grand, because it calls the roll of a long line of heroes who, animated by a love of liberty and country, offered their lives in its defence—sealing their devotion with their blood, than which nobler never flowed in the veins of men. But as it is hardly probable that I shall be able to be present on that occasion, I beg to be excused from being counted on to speak.

Thanking you for your kind remembrance of me, and wishing a most complete and grand success, and all a pleasant Reunion, I am,

Yours very truly,
THOMAS E. BARKER.

LETTER FROM HON. HENRY H. HUSE.

MANCHESTER, N. H., Aug. 28, 1882.

HORACE N. COLBATH, ESQ.,—

My Dear Sir: I am in receipt of your request to respond to the patriotic sentiment, "The soldier sons of old Barnstead," enclosed therein, at the Barnstead Reunion on the 30th inst.

I regret exceedingly my inability to comply therewith, for reasons entirely out of my power to control.

If any man in the world knows the metal of Barnstead boys in the face of the enemy, I am that one; if any one has a lasting and fervent veneration for their heroism and bravery, I am that one.

I have tramped, camped, and fought with them, and have mingled my tears with theirs over the grave of many a poor comrade who was not permitted to return to participate in your Reunion.

I have shared in their pleasures around the far-off campfire, and in the deprivations, sufferings, and miseries such as only a veteran can appreciate.

The sentiment which you ask me to answer, recalls a flood of tender memories and personal recollections, and I would gladly embrace the opportunity you offer me to pay a worthy tribute to the living and to the dead, who did honor to the goodly reputation of old Barnstead in the war of the rebellion.

I would bring to this Reunion the dying message of a typical " soldier son " of our grand old town, delivered to me in the hospital at New Orleans, after months of suffering following the battle in which he was fatally wounded. In the face of certain death, he said : " It's all right, Captain. Tell my friends at home *I fell right under the old flag*, and that is glory enough for me."

Such were the " grandsons in the Rebellion." If the " sons of 1812," and the " fathers in the Revolution," were fit sires of such as these, then truly " the love of liberty constrained them," and we do well to perpetuate their valorous deeds for the emulation of future generations.

I am very sincerely yours,

HENRY H. HUSE.

10th SENTIMENT:

The birthplaces of our fathers—Portsmouth and Newington — names as familiar as household words to every child of Barnstead ; may peace and prosperity be in their borders.

The Secretary read the following:

HYMN.—Tune: "America."

BY MRS. DARIUS FRINK, NEWINGTON, N. H.

[Written for the Barnstead Reunion.]

We welcome one and all,
At this reunion call,
    This festive day;
We'll lift our hearts with praise,
To Thee, O Strength of Days,
And sing our songs and lays,
    With melody.

We've come from many a clime,
To have a merry time,
    To greet you here;
Every familiar spot—
Hill, valley, and the cot,
No scenes have been forgot,
    To us so dear.

The dearest place on earth,
Is that which gave us birth,
    The Old Homestead;
Where we were loved so well—
By Father, Mother, Friend;
No tongue can ever tell
    How much they loved.

Many have passed away,
Since our last gala day—
    To that blest home.
They've gone where all is bright,
Where there is no more night,
For God is the great light,
    Heav'n to illume.

Our pastor, where is he?
Who taught us piety,
    With God abides.
He kept our village school,
Learnt us the Golden Rule,
Spared not the rod or 'rule
    When us he chide.

How good, O God, to spare,
With Thy omniscient care,
    Our lives so frail;
We'll worship, while we live,
Thou whom didst being give,
O may we with Thee live,
    Within the vail.

Our parents, they have gone
To swell that endless throng
    Above the skies.
We soon shall join them there,
Seraphic pleasures share—
Forever in God's care,
    In Paradise.

And as we take our leave,
Our kind regards receive,
    For courtesy.
When pass'd the last milestone,
Our eyes we'll fondly turn
On Barnstead, the hearthstone
    Of infancy.

11th SENTIMENT:

The host of men whose lives have been made better and happier by choosing for wives, daughters of old Barnstead.

Responded to by Howard A. Dodge, Esq., of Concord, N. H.

12th SENTIMENT:

The social history and reminiscences of Barnstead.

Hon. John G. Sinclair eloquently and wittily responded to this sentiment, the following being but a small part of his address, which elicited the heartiest enthusiasm and laughter. Mr. Sinclair, upon being introduced as the "Barnstead Boy" and the "wit of the family," said:

Mr. President, Ladies and Gentlemen:

Standing here in the midst of the scenes, and surrounded by the friends, of my childhood, I feel indeed, that

> "My foot is on my native heath."

Time rolls back, and boy again I gaze upon that peaceful river, hunt the turtle's nest upon its banks, and pluck from its bosom the beautiful lily.

From the time I passed the boundary of the old town, till my arrival here, memories long sleeping came leaping forth to greet me.

From the bridge which crossed its first brook, how often had I watched the trout, the dace, the roach, and the barbel, and with my pin hook *almost* caught them. That brook, upon whose green banks I once verily believed fairies, clothed in crimson and green, violet and gold, came forth at midnight to dance in the light of the moon; for did not Polly Nutter tell me so? And often did I steal from my bed in the "wee sma'" hours of the night, and from my window overlooking that brook, look and listen. But it was always a bad night for fairies, and Polly explained that, doubtless, on these particular nights, they had been detailed by their queen to watch over good little boys, who, having said their prayers on retiring, had gone immediately to sleep.

To-day, when knowledge with relentless hand has despoiled its shores of its fairies, when no more

> "Merry elves their morrice pacing
> To aerial minstrelsy;"

yet, in the music of its rippling waters, I still hear the wild refrain,

> "Men may come and men may go,
> But I go on forever,"

The Parade ground, with its green sward bespangled and bedecked with dandelion, butter-cup, and thistle-blow, is the same as when upon it I drove my hoop, chased the butterfly, and made my first acquaintance with the " business end " of the bumble-bee.

There, too, to my shame be it said, my cousin John Elbridge Bunker received at the hands of our sainted but near-sighted grandmother a whipping to which doubtless I had best title; nearly of an age and size, through a fancy of our mothers we were dressed alike; I boarded with the good old lady while attending the village school; after troubling her much, she exacted a promise that I would not stop after school was dismissed to play ball; for two long days I kept that promise, but on the third the enticement of the great national game was too much for my moral stamina.

For half an hour I engaged in it,—was at the bat, when I saw the dear old lady coming, with one hand suspiciously concealed under her apron.

A very short process of reasoning led me to the logical conclusion, that in that hand, must I confess it? was an old and not too pleasant acquaintance of mine, a well-seasoned birch stick; as she came around one side of the old church, with a brief excuse I handed the bat to my cousin and disappeared by the other, when the old lady cautiously advancing seized him by the collar and administered to my profoundly astonished cousin a castigation, which in the base ball parlance of to-day might be called a " red hot one," and when she returned to the house and found me unwhipped, I shall never forget the attitude she struck, nor her exclamation of " Mercy on me, who *have* I whipped !"

There, too, was enacted one of the most ludicrous scenes in the life of old Jonathan Scriggins, always witty, drunk or sober. Parson George had a cow which he was wont to let run in the road. She plundered indiscriminately all the carts and wagons of the farmers who came to the Parade to trade. But so long as it was Parson George's cow, it was all right. At that time, brass balls for cattle's horns first came in style. The worthy Parson, seeing some at Concord, bought a pair, brought them home, and next morning placed them on the horns of his cow, and turned her again into the road. At about eleven o'clock that morning, when several of the principal men of the town, including Parson George, were standing in front of the post-office, awaiting the arrival of the mail, the cow was observed coming down street, and Mr. Scriggins with a load on which it had evidently been better for him to have gone twice after, came staggering up street. Neither seemed disposed to give way to the other, and the cow advancing to within about four feet of him stopped short. The old gentleman, discovering that something obstructed his way, brought himself to a balance, opened wide his eyes, took in the situation, and politely removing his hat, exclaimed : " Good mornin'—hic—good mornin', madam ; I should advise you—hic—to sell your jewels and buy you a pasture !"

What fable of Æsop's ever had better moral than this ?

Sir, I have stood upon the soil of most of the states of the union. Nowhere else has the air seemed so pure, the water so limpid, the grass so green, the flowers so bright, and the hearts of men and women so loyal and true, as here in the home of our childhood.

And sir, the Hodgdons, the Nutters, the Clarks, the Bunkers, the Bickfords, the Walkers, the Jewetts, the Peaveys, the Wilsons, Garlands, Colbaths, Dows, Drews, Websters, Berrys, and Munseys, and a host of other good men and true of that day, may it please God that other generations of the sons and daughters of old Barnstead, who may meet as we now meet, may say of us as truthfully as we of them, they acted well their part, and

"After life's fitful fever they sleep well."

But time admonishes me I must close. God bless the old homestead! With pride to-day we point to her record. She has furnished the pulpit with sincere and eloquent divines, to the bench a most able jurist, to the bar most accomplished advocates, to the medical profession skilled physicians, and in times of national difficulty and danger the steps of her sons " have always been quick and to the front." On the hardest fought fields of the war of the Revolution, the war of 1812, the Mexican war, and the late war of the Rebellion, they have spilled their best blood, and offered up their lives.

13th SENTIMENT:

The resident sons and daughters of Barnstead— May they preserve unsullied its ancient reputation, keep sacred the memory of the fathers, and be always ready to welcome its wandering children to the old domain.

John B. Garland, Esq., of Barnstead, was invited to respond to this sentiment, but on account of ill-health and the infirmities of age was obliged to forego that pleasure, but answered by the following characteristic letter:

LETTER OF JOHN B. GARLAND.

NORTH BARNSTEAD, N. H., Aug. 16, 1882.

HORACE N. COLBATH, ESQ,—

Dear Sir: When I first learned there was to be a Reunion of the sons and daughters of Barnstead, it seemed that I could not deny myself the pleasure of being present on that occasion.

But a second thought convinced me that I was unable to attend. Nevertheless, I am with you in spirit.

I seem to see our guests coming from every quarter, like pilgrims to the Mecca of their early, hallowed associations and local attachments, to look once more upon the graves of their fathers, to strew them with flowers and water them with tears of love and gratitude, to revisit the ancestral hearthstone and rekindle the ancient family altar, and there make an offering of a humble and thankful heart. It is fitting, it is appropriate—there is a moral beauty in this meeting, after so long an absence. And, now they are to be here, we will kill the fatted calf and give them a hearty welcome. Doubtless many of these pilgrims have returned, like Jacob, with their pockets full of shekels. Jacob, you know, was a little tricky in his youth, but he got beat when he served fourteen years for too much wife. But in after years, when he desired to return to his Barnstead and have a reunion, and was told his brother Esau was coming to meet him, he remembered his youthful follies; so he sent before a present for a peace offering. Now, Mr. Secretary, if any of our guests should offer you a present, for love's sake take it. We can invest it in this Reunion, in Sunday-school books, in a town library, or in Paris green, for we know it is a mighty hard row to pick potato bugs for a living.

But Mr. Secretary, Barnstead has another scourge infinitely worse than bugs or army worms. It is an army of Bachelors,* who are not only destructive to potatoes, but to all hope of posterity. In my quarter of the town they are thick as toad-stools. Why, sir, a majority of our selectmen are bachelors, who ought to be fathers of the town. I do hope there will be among our guests a goodly number of marriageable ladies—each of whom will be as willing to go a courting as was Ruth, when she accepted the advice to Naomi, in the words, "All that thou sayest unto me will I do."

---

* Mr. Garland is a bachelor.

Ruth, you know, went a courting, had a pleasant interview, got a promise, and carried home nearly three pecks of barley.

May each of these marriageable ladies carry home, not a sack of barley but a live bachelor, with this promise, "All that thou sayest unto me will I do." But, whatever may be our individual circumstances, may each member of this assembly be as happy as was Joseph when he made himself known to his brethren, after he had filled their sacks with corn and money.

I close with a cordial greeting to all.

Yours truly,
JOHN B. GARLAND.

Biographical Sketches.

REV. ENOS GEORGE.

Enos George, the son of Enos and Dorothy George, was born June 2, 1781, at South Hampton, N. H.

He received his education at the town schools and at Atkinson Academy, and studied for the ministry.

At a town meeting held at Barnstead Nov. 10, 1803, it was unanimously voted to settle Mr. George as pastor. The town voted $1000 settlement and a salary. He was ordained and installed as pastor of the Congregational Church September 26, 1804, and remained pastor until his death, over fifty-five years after.

In July previous to his installation, he married Miss Sophia Chesley, daughter of Jonathan Chesley, Esq., of Barnstead. Her life was full of quiet benevolence and kindness, and adorned by Christian graces. She died February 13, 1858, aged 76 years, and was soon followed by her husband, who died October 29, 1859, aged 78 years.

For twenty years after his settlement, Parson George was teacher of the winter term of school at the Parade, and also taught several terms in the north part of the town.

From 1816 to his death in 1859, he was annually elected town-clerk of the town. That there was no opposition to his election during these forty-two years, attests the faithfulness of the officer and the popularity of the man.

In 1829, he was chaplain of the New Hampshire legislature.

In 1843 and 1844, he represented Barnstead in the general court.

While speaking of his virtues and characteristics, one is at loss where to begin and where to end.

He was well proportioned in person, erect in carriage, and of commanding presence. His countenance was grave, and gave the impression of severity; but he was quite the reverse, being cheerful and social in conversation and intercourse.

There was a vein of wit and humor in his character, which would occasionally reveal itself, but not so as to compromise his dignity and seriousness.

Wherever he was placed, or whatever his surroundings, he was always a gentleman.

As a preacher he was plain, earnest, and scriptural, seeking to present the great truths of the Bible in their simplicity. This he valued above ornament in style and oratory. Yet his rank as a pulpit orator was high. His voice was clear and sonorous, his manner and appearance dignified, his action deliberate, and his sermons models of system, scripture illustration, and good language.

His ambition was not to be a great man or preacher, but to be useful among his people, to instruct them and their children, to point out the shining way, and with them walk therein.

His ministry was long and successful. He preached 6,965 sermons, solemnized 693 marriages, and attended 1,000 funerals.

Unlike the custom of to-day, he, with his church and parish, considered his settlement final, and here his life work.

From the day he came with his young bride among them, to the day of his death, he

"Ne'er had changed, or wished to change his place."

Although his ear was open to every call of duty from abroad, and his sympathies quick to respond to all good works wherever begun or carried out, yet inside the border lines of Barnstead he saw his Master's work, and all through his long ministry his loving faith in her never knew any turning, and right generously his people repaid his love, his faith, and his labor. Probably no preacher in his day could excel Parson George in a funeral address. His services on such occasions were sought for not only by his own townsmen, but by others from abroad, members of other churches or perhaps not members of any church.

The faculty of saying the right words at the proper time, the choosing of appropriate texts of scripture, his hopeful and charitable views of the departed, and his faithful and touching admonition of the living, were peculiar gifts.

If, at such times, his strict theology yielded something to the demands of the occasion, it spoke volumes for his goodness of heart, and was gratefully remembered by the living.

The good he did, as a preacher and teacher in Barnstead, was great, and his influence for good will be felt in coming generations. He was a good man and minister, and came to his grave in a good old age, like a shock of corn fully ripe.

The memory of the just is blessed!

HON. HIRAM A. TUTTLE.

BY JOHN WHEELER, M. D.

Hiram A. Tuttle was born in Barnstead, October 16, 1837, being the elder of a family of two sons.

His father George Tuttle, and his grandfather Col. John Tuttle, were also natives of the same town. His great grandfather John Tuttle, settled in Barnstead in 1776, coming there from that locality in Dover known as "Back River," where a part of the Tuttle family had resided since the settlement there of their emigrant ancestor, John Tuttle, who came from England before 1641.

His mother, Judith Mason Davis, is a descendant from Samuel Davis, a soldier of the Revolution, and one of the primeval settlers of Barnstead. Brave soldiers of the Davis family from four generations have represented that town in the four great wars in which our country has been engaged.

When Mr. Tuttle was nine years of age, he moved with his father's family to the adjoining town of Pittsfield, where he attended the public schools and Pittsfield Academy, while the latter was under the charge successively of I. F. Folsom, Lewis W. Clark, and Prof. Dyer H. Sanborn.

After having been engaged in several vocations, in all of which he showed industry and faithfulness, at the age of seventeen years, he became connected with the clothing establishment of Lincoln & Shaw, of Concord, where he remained several years.

The ability and zeal which he exhibited while there, won for him the confidence and respect of his employers, who established him in the management of a branch store in Pittsfield, of which he soon became proprietor.

His business increased, gradually at first and then rapidly, till his establishment had gained an extensive patronage, and ranked among the largest in the state. It is so favorably remembered by former residents and patrons, that orders are received from distant states and territories.

Mr. Tuttle has also been interested in real estate. He has built many dwelling-houses, including a fine residence for himself, and the best business buildings in the village. In many ways he has promoted the growth, social and business interests, and general prosperity of his adopted town. He is a trustee in the savings bank, a director in the national bank, and a trustee of the academy in Pittsfield.

When he attained his majority, in 1859, he expressed his determination of casting his first vote with the Republican party, and has ever been true to that party. Although Pittsfield has a Democratic majority under normal circumstances, Mr. Tuttle has received the support of a large majority of its voters at times when his name has been presented for position.

In 1873 and 1874, he was representative to the legislature. In 1876, he received the appointment, with the rank of colonel, on the staff of Gov. Cheney, and with the governor and staff visited the Centennial Exhibition at Philadelphia.

He was elected a member of the executive council from the second district in 1878, and re-elected in 1879, under the new constitution, for the term of two years.

Mr. Tuttle has been very successful in all he has undertaken, but his thrift has never made him arrogant or indifferent. He has cheerfully shared with others the results of the good fortune that Providence has granted him. He is an honorable, agreeable, and companionable gentleman in all the relations of life.

As a citizen, neighbor, and friend, he is held in the highest estimation. He has furnished employment for many; and has been kind to the poor, very respectful to the aged, charitable to the erring, and a sympathizing helper to the embarrassed and unfortunate.

Few men have more or firmer personal friends, whose friendship is founded on kindness and substantial favors received. He gives with remarkable generosity to all charitable objects presented to him, and is very hospitable in his pleasant home.

Mr. Tuttle accepts the Christian religion, and worships with the Congregational church. While he contributes liberally for the support of the denomination of his choice, he does not withhold a helping hand from the other religious sects in his town.

In his domestic relations he has been very fortunate. He married, in 1859, Miss Mary C. French, the only child of John L. French, Esq., formerly cashier of the Pittsfield Bank. Their only child, Hattie French Tuttle, was born Jan. 17, 1861.

COL. E. S. NUTTER.

Eliphalet Simes Nutter, the second son of Eliphalet and Lovey (Locke) Nutter, was born in Barnstead, November 26, 1819.

He was a grandson of Major John Nutter, who settled in Barnstead in 1767, and afterwards served in the Revolution, as Major of Col. George Reid's Regiment. His father as well as his grandfather were prominent in the affairs of the town, and held the various offices in the gift of their townsmen.

His boyhood was spent on his father's farm, and his active mind and feet kept busy, as boys were wont to be in those days, helping in the cares and labor incident to a large farm.

He received the usual school advantages, and taught school several winters. Among his pupils were Hon. J. Horace Kent, Hon. C. M. Murphy, and Horace N. Colbath, Esq., who will each testify to his tact and faithfulness as a teacher.

Like his ancestors, he early evinced a taste for military affairs, and was commissioned by Gov. Isaac Hill, in 1837, a lieutenant, and by Gov. John Page, in 1839, a captain in the New Hampshire militia.

In 1844, he opened a country store at Barnstead Parade, and for eleven years did a large and increasing business. Was postmaster there eight years, and is remembered by his patrons and business associates as an honorable, keen, sagacious business man.

In 1855, he removed to Concord, N. H., where he has since resided.

Was for five years in business in New York city. Was President of the N. H. Central R. R.; owned for seven years one of the best grocery stores in Lawrence, Mass; was in the drug business in Concord five years; at present has a store on Washington St., Boston, Mass.

Since 1844 he has been in active business, and now is in the enjoyment of the accumulations of forty years' successful business—the just reward of industry, enterprise, and perseverance.

Col. Nutter has always been noted for his love of his native town; anything that concerned her good name, that tended to her material prosperity or her moral and social welfare, has enlisted his sympathy and commanded his active, substantial support.

To him, more than any other, are due the thanks of the sons and daughters of Barnstead for the Barnstead Reunion.

Upon his call, was held the meeting of the sons and daughters of Barnstead living in Concord, which resulted in the Reunion held at Phenix Hotel, Feb. 28, 1878, at which he presided; and that Reunion paved the way for the Barnstead Reunion held Aug. 30, 1882, to which he generously contributed.

He married, in 1845, Miss Sylvania M. Blanchard, of Lowell, Mass.—a true helpmeet and a worthy wife, who gracefully dispenses the hospitalities of their beautiful home.

JOHN G. SINCLAIR.

Richard Sinclair was one of the earliest settlers of the town of Gilmanton, N. H., and it is claimed that he built the first framed house there. He was a soldier in both the French and Indian war and the war of the Revolution. In the last he ranked captain, although he was generally known in the locality in which he lived as Col. Sinclair. He married Polly Cilley, a sister of Col. Joseph Cilley. Richard Sinclair, Jr., their eldest son, and one of the earliest settlers in Barnstead, was also a soldier in the war of the Revolution, and an ensign in his father's company. He married Betsey Hodgdon. Charles G. Sinclair was their only

son, who, at the age of seventeen, enlisted as a soldier in the war of 1812, and for a time was clerk for Gen. Ripley. He received a severe gunshot wound near the right lung, at the sortie at Fort Erie, which disabled him for life. He married Martha G. Norris, a daughter of Joseph Norris, of Barnstead.

John G. Sinclair, their only child, and the subject of this sketch, was born at Barnstead Parade, March 25, 1826. His father died July, 1834, leaving him and his mother in destitute circumstances. His mother, with her needle, supported them and kept him at school at Pittsfield Academy until he was thirteen years of age, when he entered the service of Webster & Peavey, merchants at Landaff, N. H. The firm consisted of Hon. Samuel Webster, of North Barnstead, and Samuel P. Peavey, a former resident of Barnstead, who married a sister of Mrs. Sinclair's.

He remained at Landaff six years, attending five terms of the Newbury Seminary, in Vermont, where he fitted for college under the tuition of Bishop Baker and Rev. Clark T. Hinman. A fear of leaving his mother destitute in case of his own death, prevented his entering college, and he commenced business for himself in a restaurant, at the corner of Hanover and Elm streets, Manchester, N. H. Not satisfied with the business, he left Manchester, and established an auction and commission business at Lawrence, Mass. Having acquired limited means, he returned to New-Hampshire, established a country store, and engaged in the manufacture of starch in Bethlehem, in 1847.

In 1852, '53, '54, and '55, in 1862 and '63, and in 1875, '76, and '77, he represented Bethlehem in the state legislature, and served as its member in the last constitutional convention.

In 1873, he represented Littleton in the legislature being then a resident of that town.

He was appointed bank commissioner by Gov. Baker, and served until the American party came into power.

In 1858 and '59, he was Senator from the 12th senatorial district, composed of Grafton and Coos counties.

He was Democratic candidate for speaker of the house, and Democratic candidate for governor in 1866, '67, and '68. Under the instruction of the convention which nominated him in 1867, he invited Gen. Walter Harriman, the Republican candidate for governor, to a public discussion of the issues involved in the campaign, the result of which was thirteen joint discussions at the principal points in the state, the first of the kind ever held in New England. In 1868, he was chairman of the N. H. delegation to the national convention. In 1876, he was Democratic candidate for United States senator, against Edward H. Rollins, Republican.

In 1879, he removed to Orlando, Orange county, in the state of Florida, where he has established a large real estate business, and is also engaged in

the cultivation of oranges and other semi-tropical fruits.

Mr. Sinclair has been twice married: first, in 1847, to Tamar M., daughter of Col. David Clark, of Landaff, by whom he had three children— Charles A., Emma S., and Martha A. Sinclair. His first wife dying, he married, in 1872, Mary E. Blandin, daughter of John Pierce, Esq., of Littleton.

COL. M. V. B. EDGERLY.

Martin Van Buren Edgerly was born in Barnstead, September, 26, 1833, the son of the late Samuel J. and Eliza (Bickford) Edgerly.

His father, a man of intelligence and mental activity, was honored by the town with several important offices, and would have been one of the foremost men in the town and prominent in the state, had not disease laid its hand on him in his early manhood.

His mother was the daughter of Moses Bickford, an early settler in Barnstead, and a very intelligent and capable woman.

When twelve years of age, his parents removed to Manchester, N. H., and he attended the public schools for several years, after which he entered the employ of the Amoskeag Manufacturing Company. At the age of twenty-three, he opened a drug store in Manchester. A year among the drugs and chemicals satisfied him of his inaptitude for trade, and he removed to Pittsfield, N. H., and soon engaged in the fire and life insurance business.

Here he made his first real beginning in life. His ready intelligence, earnestness of purpose, and personal magnetism, were requisites for success, and he built up a large business.

Having received the offer of a large salary for those times, to devote his attention exclusively to the interests of the Massachusetts Mutual Life Insurance Company, he relinquished his fire agency and went into the profession of life insurance with such energy and success as to place his company in the front rank of those doing business in New Hampshire.

One year after, in 1860, he became general agent for New Hampshire, with head-quarters at Manchester, and soon after established his residence there, which residence he still retains.

In 1863, the whole business of the company in New Hampshire, Vermont, and northern New York was committed to his care.

From 1868 to 1870, he served as superintendent of agencies throughout the United States, besides retaining the direction of his own special department.

In 1874, he was prevailed upon to give a portion of his time to the Boston office, the oldest and most important of its agencies.

He became, in 1882, one of the directors of the company, and, in 1883, was made vice-president and general manager of agencies, which position he now holds, still retaining the personal management of the New Hampshire agency.

Although the activities of his career have denied him opportunity for seeking distinction, he has ever taken a strong interest in political matters, and has been valiant in the Democratic faith.

In 1871, he was appointed by Gov. Weston chief of his military staff, with rank of colonel.

In 1872, he was delegate at large to the national Democratic convention.

Was a member of the national Democratic committee from 1872 to 1876.

In 1874, was elected one of the board of aldermen in a strong Republican ward. He frequently served as a member of the Democratic state committee, and was treasurer of the same in 1873 and 1874.

In 1882, was the Democratic candidate for governor. For once the people sought the candidate, not the candidate the nomination. He made a splendid run. Such was his popularity where he was best known that he carried Manchester, overcoming 700 Republican majority at the preceding election, carrying Hillsborough county and wiping out its 1600 adverse majority.

Besides his professional and political engagements, which would seem sufficiently numerous and complicated to engage the time of one individual, he has given the benefit of his sagacity and judgment to several commercial and financial institutions and corporations.

In 1873 and 1874, he was commander of the Amoskeag Veterans.

During the Centennial Exhibition at Philadelphia he was, by appointment of President Grant, one of the commissioners representing New Hampshire.

He was married, in 1854, to Alvina Barney, of Danbury, N. H., and has two children—Clinton Johnson (a practicing lawyer in Boston) and Mabel Clayton Edgerly.

Though in the prime of life, Col. Edgerly has done a long life-work. Yet he seems to be but on the threshold of his career. Col. Edgerly is of strong, well-built frame, with a tendency to portliness. His face is frank and pleasant, and his manners suave and engaging.

In his family and in society he elicits most cordial affection and regard, and, in business, his straightforward and inflexible conduct have made his name a synonym for probity and honor.

HON. CHARLES M. MURPHY.

We live in days when the success of men apparently born to lives of grinding toil is a frequent sign of the times.

Such opportunities are now open to him who has a good order of ability, with high health and spirits, who has all his wits about him and feels the circulation of his blood and the motion of his

heart, that the lack of early advantages forms no barrier to success.

A striking illustration of the truth of these statements is exhibited in the following sketch:

Charles M. Murphy, son of John and Mary (Meader) Murphy, was born in Alton, N. H., November 3, 1835. In 1842, his parents removed to Barnstead, and settled upon the Tasker farm at South Barnstead. Here the child grew in stature and filled out and braced his frame by hard manual labor.

Scanty record is left of these years of severe work and continuous struggle, but there is little doubt that the discipline developed an indomitable will and sturdy self-reliance, which alone enable poor men's children to grapple with the world that under more favorable circumstances might never have shown their full capacity of force and tenacity.

Again, it is widely believed, and nowhere more strongly than in opulant cities and busy marts, that a boy is better bred on a farm in close contact with the ground than elsewhere. He is quite as likely to be generous, brave, humane, honest and straightforward, as his city-bred contemporary, while as to self-dependence, strength and stamina, he has a great advantage over his rival.

He attended the district school during the winter terms until of an age suitable to leave the parental care, when for two terms he enjoyed the advantages of Norwich Academy, Vt. At school he was diligent and ambitious, cheerful and active in athletic sports.

Being the oldest of four boys, he assisted for some years his father in educating and advancing the interests of his brothers. One brother, John E., became a dentist, and practiced at Pittsfield, N. H., and Marblehead, Mass., dying at the age of thirty-five years. Another brother, Frank Murphy, M. D., a graduate of Dartmouth College, practiced in Northwood and Strafford, N. H., but died at the very flush and promise of life, aged twenty-nine. Another, Albert Warren Murphy, D. D. S., a graduate of the Philadelphia Dental College. After one year's practice in Boston, removed, in 1872, to Paris, France, where his professional labors brought him both credit and profit. At the expiration of two years, an active interest in Spanish affairs and a desire to test the business advantages of the country led him to Spain. He soon settled in Madrid, where he now resides, and in 1879 was appointed dentist to the royal family.

At the age of twenty-two he married Miss Sabrina T. Clark, daughter of Isaac Clark, Esq., of Barnstead and after a few months spent in farming on his own account, he moved to Dover, N. H., where with less than one hundred and fifty dollars he began the study of dentistry with Dr. Jefferson Smith. To this business he brought the same energy and power to prolong the hours of labor, and in two years was pronounced competent to practice. Soon after Dr. Smith died, and Dr. Murphy succeeded to his practice, and for eighteen years devoted his entire time and strength to a large and profitable business.

In 1878, he withdrew from his profession and became a broker. His coolness, sagacity and devotion to business has met well deserved success.

Dr. Murphy early gave much attention to political matters. A strong and devoted Republican, his influence in his adopted city has long been felt.

In 1871 and 1873, he was a representative from Dover, and a member of Gov. Straw's staff.

He was appointed and confirmed consul to Moscow but declined.

In 1880, was a delegate to the Republican national convention at Chicago, where he strongly supported Blaine.

In 1880, was elected mayor of the city of Dover, and re-elected in 1881.

In 1881, received the honorary degree of A. B., from Lewis College.

Dr. Murphy was elected president of the Dover Five Cent Savings Bank and under his guidance it became strong and successful.

He has been twice married. His first wife dying—being preceded to the better land by their three children,—he married Mrs. Eliza T. Hanson, widow of the late John T. Hanson of Dover, who dispenses a gracious hospitality in their spacious home.

JUDGE LEWIS W. CLARK.

Lewis Whitehouse Clark was born August 19, 1828, at Barnstead, N. H.

He is the son of Jeremiah and Hannah (Whitehouse) Clark, and has one sister, Sarah M., wife of Samuel E. Batchelder, Esq., of Illine, Ill.

The Clark family were early and influential settlers in Barnstead and prominent in its affairs.

His father, Jeremiah Clark, Esq., held many offices of trust in Barnstead, and after his removal to Pittsfield, N. H., was for many years one of its selectmen and represented it in the general court.

He acquired his preliminary education in the public schools of Barnstead and in the academies at Pittsfield and Atkinson, and then entered Dartmouth College, where he graduated in 1850.

From August, 1850, to December, 1852, he was principal of the Academy at Pittsfield.

Meanwhile he studied law; at first with Hon. Moses Norris, and afterward with A. F. L. Norris at Pittsfield, and was admitted to the Belknap county bar, from the office of the latter, Sept. 3, 1852.

He then began the practice of his profession at Pittsfield, and continued there until April 2, 1860, when he removed to Manchester, and formed a partnership with Hon. G. W. Morrison and the Hon. Clinton W. Stanley.

In November, 1866, he dissolved his connection with them, and practiced alone for a year or two, and then associated himself with Henry H. Huse, continuing this partnership till May 24, 1872, when he was appointed attorney general of New Hampshire, to fill the vacancy caused by the death of Hon. William C. Clarke.

He was appointed judge of the supreme court of New Hampshire August 13, 1877, which position he now holds.

He represented Pittsfield in the state legislature in 1856 and 1857, and was the nominee of the Democratic party for member of congress in the second district in 1865.

Mr. Clark married, December 29, 1852, Miss Helen M., daughter of the late Capt. William Knowlton, of Pittsfield, by whom he has one daughter, Mary Helen, and a son, John L.

Few men in New Hampshire have so many warm personal friends as the subject of this sketch. A very liberal man, of patriotic and high-toned impulses, he is widely known and esteemed. He has no superior in the state as a ready, off-hand speaker. Felicitous in language, eloquent in thought, and generous in every impulse, he is an admirable advocate before a jury, and wherever he appears as a public speaker acquits himself with signal ability.

As a judge he has won the confidence of his associates on the bench, of the bar of the state, and of the people, who recognize in him an honest and just judge.

HON. JOHN P. NEWELL.

[TAKEN FROM THE HISTORY OF MANCHESTER.]

John Plumer Newell was born in Barnstead, July 29, 1823.

He is the son of William H. and Olive (Dennett) Newell, and is one of thirteen children, all but two now living. Mr. Newell spent his early life upon his father's farm, acquiring an education in the district and select schools taught in town, and fitting for college at the academies at Rochester, Pittsfield, and Gilmanton.

He entered Dartmouth college in 1845, and graduated in 1849, at the head of his class. After graduating he taught the academy at Pittsfield, studying law meanwhile with A. F. L. Norris till March, 1851, when he went to Manchester to take charge of the high school there, which he taught till the summer term of 1853. He then resumed the study of law in the office of S. H. & B. F. Ayer, of that city, and was admitted, in August, 1853, to the Hillsborough bar.

Early in the winter of 1853 he opened an office in Manchester, and continued in the practice of his profession till the spring of 1855, when he resumed charge of the high school, continuing its principal till the fall of 1862.

In May, 1863, he became principal of Pinkerton academy, at Derry, N. H., and held the position till the summer of 1865, when he returned to Manchester, where he has since made his home, being engaged in general business.

While at Derry, Mr. Newell had application to take charge of Appleton academy at New Ipswich, N. H., the boys' high school, the girls' high school, and the Putnam free school at Newburyport, Mass., but, having decided to quit teaching, he declined them all.

Mr. Newell was elected by the city councils, in February, 1873, mayor of Manchester, and was one of its representatives in 1872, 1874, and 1875.

He was elected, in 1856, president of the first Young Men's Christian Association in the city of Manchester, and served one year; and soon after the Association was re-organized, in 1868, he was again elected its president, and held the office six consecutive years.

He has been, since 1872, deacon of the First Congregational church in Manchester; for ten years was president of the society connected with the church, and for the same number of years superintendent of its Sunday school.

In 1880, Mr. Newell was chosen cashier of the Derry National Bank, and soon after was appointed assignee of the Derry Savings Bank.

He is at the present time one of the trustees of Pinkerton academy at Derry, N. H., which has a fund of nearly $250,000, and is a member of the board of trustees of the Elliott hospital in Manchester.

Mr. Newell married, August, 1855, Mary W., only daughter of the late Chief Justice Samuel D. Bell, by whom he had one child who died in infancy. His first wife died August, 1859, and he married, June, 1863, Elizabeth M., daughter of Hon. T. T. Abbott, formerly mayor of Manchester, by whom he has one child, Mary Bell, now living.

Mr. Newell is a fine scholar, a Christian gentleman, and a pleasant, agreeable man. He has always, whether mayor of the city, teacher of the high school, or president of the Young Men's Christian Association, exerted an elevating influence upon those with whom he has come in contact.

JOHN HORACE KENT.

John Horace Kent, whose life-like portrait precedes this sketch, was the only son of John Kent, a native of Rochester, New Hampshire, who, after a few years' residence in early life in Portsmouth, N. H., married Ruhamah Dearborn, daughter of Asa Dearborn, of that town and removed to Barnstead, in 1823, where the subject of this article was born, October, 10, 1828.

John Horace attended the Pittsfield and Strafford academies, the Portsmouth high school (at the time John True Tasker, of Barnstead, was the principal), and in 1843, the year in which his father died, he with his mother removed to New Bedford, Mass., and became a member of the high school in that city.

In 1845, he went to New York to enter a wholesale establishment, remaining therein two years, performing most efficient service for his

employers. He afterward was engaged in the steam tannery business in western Pennsylvania with his uncle.

In 1849, at the breaking out of the California gold fever, Mr. Kent withdrew from the tannery business in order to go to the land of promise, and while en route, being detained in Panama for a few weeks, he commenced the publication of a newspaper called the *Panama Star*, which proved a successful venture, and up to the present time has held a leading position among the newspapers of the day. Disposing, finally, of his interest therein, Mr. Kent went to San Francisco, where his abilities were quickly recognized, soon giving him many positions of prominence, among them a director of the "Society of California Pioneers," a member of the first "Committee of Vigilance," which was organized in June, 1851, and whose record has become an interesting part of the history of California; he was also made secretary of the Broderick wing of the Democratic committee of San Francisco, held an important government position under President Pierce in the Customs Department, and lastly was elected coroner, a prominent and lucrative office, which latter position he held for a long time and with marked ability. During the memorable Frazer river mining excitement, he went to British Columbia as special correspondent, and also accompanied the builders of the Southern overland telegraph line, in the same capacity, in the interest of the San Francisco press. In gleaning the news of those pioneer days, he exhibited great tact, and, as the records show, always "came in ahead" of his competitors, not only in gathering up but in the early transmission of the intelligence of the day.

During his residence in California, Mr. Kent visited New England several times, and on one of these trips, December, 1852, married Miss Adeline Penniman, the youngest child of Bethuel and Sophia Penniman, of New Bedford, Mass., and then returned to the Western coast, with his estimable bride, where he remained until 1860. While sojourning on the Pacific slope, Mr. Kent, by his keen executive abilities, combined with indomitable pluck, much needed in those days, won considerable prominence; his services were in constant demand, his views were frequently sought, for in matters of polity having no sympathy with that "as-it-was-in-the-beginning-is-now-and-ever-shall-be" idea, he believed in and hailed changes which tended to improvements, and hence was rightly considered a progressive man, who knew no such word as fail,—characteristics which have followed him all through his active life. Mr. Kent returned permanently to New England in 1860, making the trip overland, a good portion of the way by stage lines, his devoted helpmeet, and son born to them in San Francisco, preceding him by steamer via Panama to New York. When the war of the Rebellion broke out, Mr. Kent becoming convinced of the righteousness of the Northern side of the dispute, volunteered his services as a private, and joined a Massachusetts regiment, going to the Department of North Carolina, thence to the Army of the Potomac. Late in 1863, he was mustered out of the service, and appointed a special agent of the provost marshal's department for the district of New Hampshire, with headquarters at Portsmouth, holding that office until it was abolished.

Mr. Kent has since that time to the present been a resident of Portsmouth, and during this period has held several offices of public trust, being twice elected city marshal and twice appointed to responsible positions in the secret service of the U. S. treasury department; also has been special officer and claim agent for the Eastern railroad, and special inspector of customs for the district of New Hampshire. In 1873 and 1874, he was elected as representative to the N. H. legislature, and appointed a member of Gov. Cheney's staff, with the rank of colonel; in 1876, was appointed sheriff of Rockingham county by the governor and council, and three times elected to the same by the people since the office has been made elective, at present holding the position, and has since the commencement of the publication of this book again been complimented with a renomination for another term of official life; also that of United States deputy marshal, with an enviable reputation in the work of investigating crime and ferretting out criminals. Col. Kent is connected with several secret bodies, including DeWitt Clinton Commandery of Knights Templar, St. Andrews Lodge, Washington Chapter, and Davenport Council of Masons, Osgood Lodge of Odd Fellows, Storer Post, No. 1, Grand Army of the Republic, and Sagamore Lodge Knights of Honor, all of Portsmouth, N. H.

Thoroughly social and free in his nature, Mr. Kent became for some years addicted to drink. His downward career seemed rapid; but at last, fully realizing that nature was giving way under these excesses, he resolved to quit the habit, and after a season of treatment at the Washingtonian Home in Boston, he came forth a thoroughly reformed man, and afterward held the presidency of the Washingtonian Total Abstinence Society of Portsmouth, the same office in the New England Reformed Men's Association, and of the New Hampshire State Temperance Association.

He inaugurated a series of temperance meetings in various parts of the state, and was the principal speaker therein, the happy results of these meetings being marked by the reclaiming of many hard drinkers, who are to-day blessing "Horace Kent" for his noble and unremitting work in their behalf,—a work more blessed because his own bitter experience had been his teacher. In years of his greatest tribulation, brought on solely by drink, Col. Kent had the unswerving love and trust of a noble, devoted wife and mother whose efforts to reclaim him were as unceasing as hope, and at last, after the most bitter agonies of spirit, the fruition came,—came like a benediction, for the salvation was complete and life to each became a new song,—a "*te deum.*"

Col. Kent has an only son, Horace Penniman Kent, who occupies a government position in Boston, and who possesses in a marked degree the excellent qualities of his devoted parents.

Hosts of friends, scattered from Maine's rockbound coast to California's golden shores, attest to virtues which ennoble and distinguish character, to generosity and benevolence which abound almost to a fault, and bear willing testimony to the fidelity, zeal, and earnestness which has followed the performance of every trust, to the liberality, faithfulness, and ready support given every measure conducive to the welfare of the community, and lastly, to the unswerving friendship of John Horace Kent.

DR. JOSEPH R. HAYES.
BY ROBERT B. CAVERLY.

Joseph R. Hayes was born in Barnstead, March 7, 1818. His father was Lemuel, son of Paul Hayes, late of Alton, N. H., who was of Scotch origin, and whose father was one of the early settlers of New England.

His mother was Abigail, daughter of John Bennet, of New Durham, N. H. His parents were married in 1800, and had nine children, seven sons and two daughters.

The father failing in the farming business, and the mother dying, the children were early left without care and the means of support.

From this cause the subject of this sketch was consigned to the care of his revered grandparents. He was limited in his school advantages, and at the age of seventeen became a student at the Free Baptist Institution at Strafford, N. H., now known as Austin academy. Here he was fellow-student with Henry Wilson, afterwards Vice-President of the United States, and also with Zachariah B. Caverly, afterwards an able lawyer and secretary of legation to the republic of Peru. Both remained his cordial friends all their days.

From the academy he became a teacher, first in 1838 and 1839 at Farmington and Dover, N. H., and then in 1840, at Wilmington, Delaware, where he remained until 1847, and while teaching he pursued the study of medicine.

Leaving Wilmington, he returned to New England, and, uniting in marriage with the amiable Leah D., daughter of Paul Hayes, Esq., of Alton, he established himself in the business of a druggist and apothecary in the city of Lowell, Mass., where ever since he has diligently and successfully prosecuted his profession up to a good name and fame, and to an independent fortune. Dr. Hayes had three children, but lost them in their infancy. The dear wife and mother died in 1874.

In course of time, Feb. 1883, the Doctor intermarried with Mrs. Mary White Leighton, a lady of much amiability, and now in the full promise of a continued useful and successful life, he occupies his stately granite mansion, on the lofty banks of the Merrimack, overlooking its limpid waterfalls and its progressive spindle city. Dr. Hayes was the leading man, who by a generous contribu-

tion and otherwise induced the writer of this to undertake the compilation of the History of Barnstead out of the material which had previously been collected by the late Dr. J. P. Jewett—a history illustrated and poetized so it is now valued and advertised in Boston at the price of $5 per copy.

The Doctor, although always absorbed in his professional duties, has often been called by his fellow-citizens to important places of trust, and sometimes he has found time for such duties. He has been a director of the city library, is one of the trustees of the Lowell cemetery, and a trustee in the Central Savings Bank in Lowell. He was one of the founders and is a director in a large literary society in Middlesex county, Mass., for the advancement of science and art, under the corporate name of "THE LITERATI."

Endowed with that equal disposition which always creates its own happiness, and with that open and flowing benevolence which always promotes the happiness of others, may the Doctor, with his lovely lady, long live and faithfully in his sphere continue to adorn his profession, and to the end of life nobly fulfil the mission of his manhood.

HANSON CAVERNO CANNEY, M. D.

Dr. Canney is the son of Paul J. and Eliza (Hanson) Canney, both natives of Barnstead.

The Canney and Hanson families were among the early settlers of Dover, N. H., and zealous and respectable members of the Society of Friends, who patiently bore their part in the religious persecutions of Governor Wentworth, and each suffered in the long and bloody Indian wars, during which one-twelfth of the inhabitants of the province were either killed or carried captives to Canada. Through these trying periods they proved by their acts the steadfastness of their faith, although Jeremy Belknap, in the second volume of his "Early History of New Hampshire," remarks of one of them that "having several lusty sons, and always keeping their guns loaded for *game*, the Indians kept away from him."

Dr. Canney was born in the immediate neighborhood of Mount Job, North Strafford, New Hampshire, November 17, 1839, and lived there until his parents removed to Barnstead, to the homestead of his grandfather, Caverno Hanson, Esq., when he was seven years of age.

He assisted his parents upon the farm and was a pupil in the common schools until old enough to attend a preparatory school, when he fitted for college at Pittsfield, New Hampton, and Gilmanton academies.

After teaching in various places, he studied medicine with John Wheeler, M. D., of Pittsfield, and Prof. A. B. Crosby, of Hanover, N. H., graduating from Dartmouth Medical College in the class of 1864.

He married, Nov. 13, 1864, Ellen M. Nutter, the daughter of Wm. P. and Hannah (Chesley) Nutter. The Nutter family was among the first settlers of that part of Dover known as "Bloody Point Parish," afterward incorporated under the name of Newington, and came early to Barnstead.

He has been blessed with two children, Bertie Caverno, who lived but a few months, and Grettie Eliza, now aged 7 years.

On Jan. 1, 1865, Dr. Canney commenced the practice of medicine at Auburn, N. H., as successor of the venerable Nathan Plumer, M. D. There upon the shore of the beautiful Lake Massabesic the first ten years of his married life were passed in the successful practice of his profession.

He devoted a portion of his time to writing for several papers and magazines, but under various *nom de plumes*, for the Doctor thought and still thinks that the public consider the man who writes poetry a wild dreamer,—hardly capable of the careful and exact reasoning needful for the practice of medicine.

During the larger part of his residence in Auburn he was superintendent of schools; in 1873 and 1874, represented Auburn in the legislature; was two years a censor of the N. H. Medical Society and first vice-president of the North Rockingham Medical Association.

In November, 1874, he removed to Manchester, and purchased, in connection with J. A. Wiley, Esq., the City Hall drug store, also opening an office at No. 7, Hanover St., for the practice of his profession, where he still remains.

In 1875 and 1876 he was city physician, and in 1876 represented his ward in the legislature. In

1878, finding some objectionable features in the drug business, he sold his interest and gave his entire time to his profession.

In 1881, he purchased an interest in and became editor of the literary paper known as " *The Girls and Boys of New Hampshire*," but finding, after one year, that his literary and professional duties were more laborious than he anticipated, he disposed of the paper, devoting his undivided attention since to his increasing practice.

DR. GEORGE W. EMERSON.

George Washington Emerson, son of Solomon and Deborah Emerson, was born in Barnstead October 25, 1823. The family were among the first and foremost of those who reclaimed Barnstead from the primeval forest.

He attended the public schools of Barnstead, where he was a close student.

In 1837, with his two older brothers, Thomas and Solomon, and his twin brother Jefferson and others, he helped organize the Barnstead Brass Band, which has had a continued active existence ever since and is now the oldest band in the United States. He was elected its leader in 1839, and served as such till 1843, when he left Barnstead for Boston, Mass., where he engaged as musician in Barnum's traveling show, continuing with it for one season.

In 1844, he went to New York city and engaged in the business of publishing maps.

He went South in 1846, to Newmarket in the valley of Virginia,—commenced the study of medicine, in 1847, with Dr. J. D. Hitt.

In 1849, went to Washington, D. C., and studied dentistry with Dr. Robert Arthur, meanwhile attending lectures in the medical department of University of Georgetown, D. C.

In 1852, he went to Philadelphia, and attended lectures in the Philadelphia College of Dental Surgery. Here his courage was severely tested. His means had become so exhausted that in order to attend lectures at this term he was obliged to take a room in an attic, and to subsist upon two cents' worth of corn meal daily, made into a mush with his own hands. But he was successful graduating with the first honors, receiving the title of D. D. S. in February, 1853.

Dr. Emerson at once located in Glassboro', N. J., and commenced the practice of dentistry.

Seeking a warmer climate, he went South, and located in Griffin, Georgia, Jan., 1855. Here he was very successful. In 1859, Dr. Emerson removed to the city of Macon, Georgia, and erected a fine brown stone front building. The upper stories he arranged with special reference to the practice of his profession, and when his dental rooms were completed, a writer in the *N. Y. Dental Journal* said: "Dr. Emerson's dental rooms in Macon, Georgia, are decidedly the best appointed, most unique, and most convenient of any in the United States."

Dr. Emerson became one of the leading dentists of the South, his fine operations attracting patients from adjoining states.

After fourteen years' successful practice in this city, his health becoming impaired he determined to rest. Renting his fine rooms to Drs. J. P. & W. R. Holmes he returned to Barnstead, Nov., 1873.

On his retiring from practice the *Macon Telegraph and Messenger* said:

"The public will have observed with regret that this distinguished dentist has retired from practice, at least for a time. Dr. Emerson is a most estimable gentleman, and has proved himself an excellent citizen of Macon. His skill in his profession has placed many of our people under personal obligations to him. He will be followed by the best wishes of the Macon public wherever he goes."

On his return to Barnstead, Dr. Emerson purchased of his brother the old homestead farm, where he was born and where his boyhood was spent, and has enlarged and refitted the buildings thereon, making a beautiful residence.

Dr. Emerson has devoted his attention in part to interests of agriculture. He was president of the Barnstead Agricultural and Mechanical Society for several years, and to his untiring efforts is largely due the success of the town fairs. He was also one of the directors of the Belknap County Agricultural Society.

In 1877 and 1878, he represented Barnstead in the legislature, and afterwards was elected to offices of trust in the town until he positively refused to serve.

Dr. Emerson, by his liberality and public spirit, has endeared himself to the citizens of Barnstead to an enviable degree. His labors and donations for everything touching the welfare or good name of Barnstead will long be remembered.

HON. GEORGE S. PENDERGAST.

George S. Pendergast, son of Deacon Solomon and Rebecca Pendergast; born Nov. 19, 1815; educated at the common schools, and at Strafford, and Gilmanton academies; went to Boston, Mass., 1837; found employment in a grocery store; was occupied as a clerk and for himself in that business, successfully, till 1844; then went to Charlestown, Mass., where he engaged in the fancy cake and pastry baking business, with success, till 1862, when he retired from active business.

Served as one of the assessors of the city of Charlestown for the years 1862 and 1863, and was elected an assessor in 1864, but declined to serve. Was a member of the Massachusetts house of representatives from the above city for the years 1864 and 1865. Was elected without his knowledge that he was to be voted for city treasurer and collector of taxes, in 1864; but owing to other duties he declined to accept the office. Was an active member of the recruiting committee during the war of the Rebellion, and, the latter part thereof, had full and exclusive charge of the enrollment lists for said city. Near the close of the war he received from the enrolled men of his ward a handsome silver service, of eleven pieces, as a testimonial of their appreciation of his services in aid of recruiting. Was elected, 1868, chairman of the board of assessors of said city, and continued to be re-elected to that office and serve therein, till the annexation of the city of Charlestown to the city of Boston, January, 1874. Has been one of the first assistant assessors of the city of Boston every year since said annexation, to and including 1883 and 1884, and is elected for 1884 and 1885. Has written several able articles on taxation, notably one on Taxation of Incomes, published by the tax commissioners of Massachusetts in the appendix of their report on taxation and exemption therefrom, in 1875. He is one of the trustees and vice-presidents and a member of the investment committee of the Charlestown Five Cent Savings Bank. On the organization of the Mutual Protection Fire Insurance Company, Charlestown, in 1864, he was elected one of the directors thereof, and continues to serve in that capacity to the present time.

The subject of this sketch desires to have herewith recorded his grateful acknowledgement of the very kind consideration received from the citizens of Charlestown and Boston, and also his abiding love toward Barnstead the home of his childhood.

HARRIET P. DAME.

Miss Harriet Patience Dame, daughter of James Chadbourne and Phebe Ayers Dame, was born at Barnstead, January 5, 1815.

Her parents moved to Barnstead about the year 1797. They then had one son. Five children were born in Barnstead, of whom Harriet was the youngest.

In 1843, she removed to Concord, N. H., with her parents, where she resided until the war of the Rebellion.

That event at once aroused her patriotism, and she anxiously desired to aid the Union cause. Not being permitted to carry a musket, she decided to become an army nurse, and joined the Second Regiment N. H. Vols., as hospital matron, in June, 1861, and remained connected with the regiment until it was finally mustered out in December, 1865—four years and eight months. The pay of a hospital matron was then six dollars per month. In 1863, it was increased to ten dollars per month, and so remained during the war.

She was in camp near Washington, D. C., till November, 1861; then at Budd's Ferry, Md., till April, 1862, went with the regiment to Yorktown and up the Peninsula. She was inside the trenches at Fair Oaks while the rebels were bombarding them, and a shell passed through the tent occupied by her.

After that battle, the Union troops retreating, she walked a long distance and assisted the sick and wounded on the march.

One very dark night she passed in the thick wood, not knowing whether she was nearer to friends or foes, and for that reason not attempting to proceed.

At this time, she was the only woman in the brigade, and frequently nursed the sick and wounded of other regiments. She was well known to all the soldiers of the brigade, and those of other regiments seemed to rival the Second in the respect shown her.

She was with her regiment at Harrison's Landing and remained there until August, 1862, when she left that place on a hospital boat and on arrival at Fortress Monroe, was ordered to accompany a ship-load of sick and wounded to New York. She rejoined her regiment at Alexandria, Aug. 23, 1862, and participated in the second Bull Run Battle, and at the retreat of the army was placed on duty as a nurse at a hospital near the old stone church at Centreville, Va..

While *en route* from that point to Washington, with sick and wounded, she was taken prisoner, but was soon released.

At the battle of Fredericksburg, in December, 1862, she suffered much from exposure, but remained with the sick and wounded until they were removed to Washington, where she accompanied them.

There, by universal consent, she assumed charge of the supplies sent from New Hampshire for the sick and wounded soldiers from that state, and distributed them to the most needy at the different hospitals.

During the winter of 1862-3 the Second Regiment was recruiting. Upon its return to active duty, Miss Dame rejoined them, and was at the battle of Gettysburg. She remained in the corps hospital until the sick and wounded were removed to the general hospital. She then rejoined the regiment at Point Lookout, where it was guarding prisoners of war.

Being worn out by exposure and incessant duty, Miss Dame was ordered South to investigate the sanitary condition of the New Hampshire troops stationed near Charleston, S. C. She sailed from New York on the steamer Argo, visited Morris and Folly Islands, *en route* to Fort Gregg, and being fired on from Fort Moultrie, returned to Hilton Head, and from there went to St. Augustine, Fla., and ascertaining the impracticability of establishing a general hospital at that point, returned North, and, at the request of Gen. Sprague, of New York, reported the condition of the sick on the boats, while *in transitu*, as observed by her, to Surgeon General Barnes, which resulted in much good to disabled soldiers who were compelled to make long journeys to reach suitable hospitals.

Miss Dame rejoined her regiment, and was at the battle of Cold Harbor. Soon after that, the original three-years men of the regiment, who had not re-enlisted, were mustered out. She remained with the re-enlisted men, and was for a time in front of Petersburg, and then at Chapin's Farm near Richmond.

About this time, the army was so continuously on the march that corps hospitals were established, and the sick and wounded sent to them until they could be safely moved to hospitals farther north.

Miss Dame was appointed matron of the 18th Corps hospital Sept., 1864, and had supervision of the nurses on duty, and also of the cooking for the sick and wounded in the hospital, which at times amounted to three thousand.

She remained there until the close of the active operations of the war, and then rejoined the 2d Regiment at Manchester, Va., opposite Richmond, and then to Fredericksburg, after which they were ordered to Richmond county, between the Potomac and the Rappahannock rivers. The regiment while there suffered more by sickness and death than during any equal time of its service.

On the the 25th of December, 1865, the regiment was mustered out of the service, and Miss Dame's army record ended with theirs. Of her services Gen. Gilman Marston, for years colonel of the regiment, has said:

"Miss Harriet P. Dame went out with the Second New Hampshire Volunteers in June, 1861, and remained with that regiment and in the army hospitals till after the close of the war. She sought no soft place, but wherever her regiment went she went, often marching on foot and camping without tent on the field. She was always present where most needed, and to the suffering, whether 'Yank' or 'Grayback,' it made no difference. She was truly an angel of mercy. Miss Dame was the bravest woman I ever knew. I have seen her face a battery without flinching, while a man took refuge behind her to avoid the flying fragments of bursting shells. Of all the men and women who volunteered to serve their country during the late war, not one is more deserving of reward than Harriet P. Dame."

After the close of the war, Miss Dame remained with friends in Washington, D. C. (her home in Concord having been broken up), until the summer of 1866, when she visited her brothers in Wisconsin and Michigan.

In August, 1867, she was appointed a clerk in the Treasury Department, at a salary of nine hundred dollars per annum, where she still remains, enjoying many proofs of the love of the soldiers, and the respect of all who know her.

MISS NANCY PENDERGAST.

Nancy Pendergast, daughter of Dea. Solomon and Rebecca Pendergast, was born at Barnstead, N. H., June 1, 1819.

She received her education at the town schools and at Pittsfield academy, and led a quiet uneventful life at home and in her brother's family at Charlestown, Mass., until the dark days of the Rebellion, when she obeyed the voice of duty and gave efficient service as a nurse in the hospitals at Point Lookout, and at Annapolis, Md.

7

In November, 1862, having decided to labor as a nurse, she applied to a friend in Charlestown, who was in communication with Miss Dorothy L. Dix, who had been appointed by the government superintendent of nurses, and learning that her services were wanted, she went to Dr. Hayward, of Boston, for approval and acceptance as hospital nurse, and also for transportation papers, and in one week after deciding to go, was on her way to Washington.

She met Miss Dix on the train between Baltimore and Washington, and accompanied her home, remaining with her that night. In the morning she was ordered to Columbia hospital, till there should be an opportunity for her to go to Point Lookout.

In about ten days Miss Dix ordered her to report to her next morning at seven o'clock.

A cattle boat was going down the Potomac to Point Lookout, on which she and another nurse who like her was waiting for transportation could go.

They were the only women on the boat, and had to accept very meagre accommodations. They were served with supper on the boat, but during the night the cattle burst through into the kitchen and no breakfast could be given. It was not until 3 o'clock P. M. that they arrived at Point Lookout, Dec. 10, 1862.

There they found plenty of work to be done. On the 15th of December, a boat load of wounded soldiers arrived from the battle of Fredericksburg, which took place the 13th.

The nurses were called on to do what they could for the poor suffering boys. As there were not surgeons enough to attend to them, immediately Miss Pendergast, with a basin of water, sponges, and bandages, dressed wound after wound, and if the gratitude of these sufferers was any proof that the work was well done, then surely it was a success.

From the battle of Gettysburg, six wounded soldiers were brought on stretchers to her ward; but in time they all recovered, ascribing their recovery in a large measure to her assiduous care.

The soldiers' aid society of Charlestown, Mass., and also private individuals sent her many generous contributions of delicacies for the sick and wounded soldiers, which were thoroughly appreciated and were very beneficial. She remained at Point Lookout till September, 1863, when she was so ill with fever and ague, that she was obliged to return to her home in Charlestown, and remained there until the next spring, when Miss Dix wrote her asking for her service again.

In April, 1864, Miss Pendergast reported to her at Washington, and was sent to Annapolis, Md., where she remained till the close of the war.

Here she saw more of suffering than ever before. The Union soldiers from the rebel prisons were landed here. Boatloads after boatloads of these poor, suffering, emaciated soldiers arrived in the most forlorn condition, many of them without hats or shoes, their clothing in rags, and so weak they could hardly walk.

It was heart-rending to listen to their stories of the terrible suffering endured in those prisons. Many of them would sink away and die, and very few probably who reached home ever fully recovered.

Since the war, Miss Pendergast has worthily filled several positions of responsibility and trust, the most note-worthy being that of housekeeper and valued friend of the late Rev. James Walker, D. D., LL. D., of Cambridge, Mass., Ex-President of Harvard College. Since his death, she has continued a life of activity and usefulness, but often visits her native town, for which she cherishes an ardent affection.

JOHN D. NUTTER.

John Dennett Nutter, the son of John Nutter, 4th, and Hannah (Dennett) Nutter, was born in Barnstead, June 4, 1812,—a few months after his father's death.

His grandfather, Benjamin Nutter, Esq., was one of the first settlers in Barnstead, and at his house was held the first town meeting in Barnstead, of which he was moderator, and was chosen one of its first selectmen, and continued as such for many years.

His father dying in early manhood, upon his mother devolved the care of the family.

The subject of this sketch remained with his mother until his fifteenth year, when he became an apprentice of his uncle, Hon. Charles Dennett,

British American Bank Note Co. Montreal

of Rochester, N. H., where he learned the cabinet maker's trade.

On attaining his majority, he worked for a time at Mont Vernon, N. H., and afterwards at Stanstead, Canada.

For one year, Mr. Nutter was engaged in the banking business in Indiana, but sold out his business and returned to Nashua, N. H., and engaged in business as a merchant. Afterwards he removed to Montreal, Canada, and became a broker, and subsequently was also largely engaged in the lumber business.

Mr. Nutter has been successful in all his business enterprises and has accumulated a large fortune.

His residence upon McGill Avenue, Montreal, among the wealthy aristocracy, is spacious and beautiful; yet therein reigns the open-hearted hospitality characteristic of a true son of old Barnstead.

Mr. Nutter married Miss Harriet Stevens, of Mont Vernon, by whom he has three sons, all living.

Accompanied by his family, Mr. Nutter visited Europe, and spent a year among the objects of interest found in the cities of the old world.

Although for many years Mr. Nutter has lived under the flag of a foreign nation, and rarely revisits his native town, yet his interest in its good name and welfare is strong and abiding, and its citizens rejoice in his prosperity, and proudly claim him as an emigrant son of old Barnstead.

CONTRIBUTIONS.

The following contributions were received from emigrant sons and daughters, and former residents of Barnstead, in aid of the Reunion:

H. A. Tuttle, Pittsfield, N. H.,	$25.00
E. S. Nutter, Concord, N. H.,	25.00
M. V. B. Edgerly, Manchester, N. H.,	25.00
C. M. Murphy, Dover, N. H.,	25.00
J. G. Sinclair, Orlando, Fla.,	25.00
Mrs. James R. Hill, Concord, N. H.,	25.00
Geo. S. Pendergast, Boston, Mass.,	10.00
B. G. Adams, Milton, N. H.,	5.00
A. G. Thompson, New York City,	5.00
S. E. Goodwin, New York City,	5.00
J. P. Newell, Manchester, N. H.,	5.00
J. D. Nutter, Montreal, Canada,	5.00
Geo. F. Knowles, Lynn, Mass.,	5.00
H. C. Canney, Manchester, N. H.,	5.00
L. G. Young, M. D., Candia, N. H.	3.00
N. G. Carr, Concord, N. H.,	3.00
Aaron Whittemore, Jr., Pittsfield, N. H.,	2.00
H. A. Dodge, Concord, N. H.,	2.00
Reuben Edgerly, Gilmanton, N. H.,	1.00
Andrew Bunker, Concord, N. H.,	1.00
N. H. Leavitt, Newmarket, N. H.,	1.00
J. B. Merrill, Concord, N. H.,	1.00

NAMES

OF

EMIGRANT SONS AND DAUGHTERS OF BARNSTEAD,

AS RETURNED BY

THE TOWN CANVASSING COMMITTEE.

[In copying we have omitted the name of the wife, where both husband and wife were natives of Barnstead. Such cases are designated by a star prefixed to the name of the husband. We are aware the list does not include all who were or should have been invited, as some names were given the Secretary in the hurry and bustle of Committee meetings, when an invitation would be forwarded but no record made of the name, address, &c., while the post-office address of others could not be obtained. We shall be agreeably surprised if there are not mistakes in the names and residences.—ED.]

Abbott, Mrs. Roger	Worcester, Mass.
Adams, P. H.	Pittsfield, N. H.
Adams, Mrs. G. A.	Boston, Mass.
Adams, Wilson N.	Pittsfield, N. H.
Adams, Alvah O.	" "
Adams, Mrs. N.	" "
Adams, Wm. C.	" "
Adams, Hannah	Lowell, Mass.
Adams, Albert	Tilton N. H.
Adams, Frank J.	Concord, N. H.
Adams, Samuel H.	Minneapolis, Minn.
Adams, Austin W.	Boston, Mass.

Adams, Mrs. Mary	Portsmouth, N. H.
Adams, Benjamin G.	Milton, "
Adams, Eben W.	" "
Adams, Nellie	" "
Adams, James	Hillsborough, "
*Aikins, Dr. F. J.	Pittsfield, "
Aikins, C. H.	Gilmanton, "
Aikins, Mrs. Annie I.	" "
Allen, C. H.	Laconia, "
Atkinson, Mrs. E.	Tilton, "
Avery, S. D. H.	Rochester, "
Avery, Samuel E.	Barrington, "
Avery, James	Rochester, "
Avery, W. M.	Farmington, "
Ayers, Mrs. D. B.	Manchester, "
*Babb, Ira	Strafford, "
Babb, Mrs. Mahala	Ashland, "
Babb, Samuel	Pittsfield, "
Babb, Darius	Georgetown, Mass.
Babb, Albert S.	Pittsfield, N. H.
Baker, Mrs. A. A.	Epsom, "
Baker, Mrs. S. R.	Walnut, Iowa.
Berry, Miss Fannie	New York City.
Berry, Charles	Dover, N. H.
Berry, Abbie	" "
Berry, Laura	" "
Berry, Mrs. Freeman	" "
Berry, Thomas	Concord, "
Berry, Fred E.	Live Oaks, Fla.
Berry, Mrs. H. O.	Alton, N. H.
*Berry, Plumer O.	Farmington, N. H.
Berry, John M.	" "
Berry, Charles H.	Middletown, Ct.
Berry, Miss Ardena	Farmington, N. H.
Berry, Mrs. E.	Dover, "

THE BARNSTEAD REUNION. 109

Berry, Alonzo — Alton, N. H.
Berry, Mrs. Francis — Roslindale, Mass.
Bean, J. P. — Alfred, Me.
Barton, J. W. — Concord, N. H.
Barton, George — Dover, "
Barker, Col. T. E. — Malden, Mass.
Bachelder, Samuel — Salem, "
Bachelder, Mrs. S. M. — Harristown, Ill.
*Bunker, Andrew — Concord, N. H.
*Bunker, Hollis — Metz, Ill.
Bunker, J. Elbridge — Kasson, Minn.
Bunker, Cyrus — Bethlehem, N. H.
Bunker, Abram — Manchester, "
Bunker, William — Bethlehem, "
Bunker, Charles — Concord, "
Bunker, Harry — Pittsfield, "
*Bunker, Prof. C. M. — Peacham, Vt.
Bunker, Asa F. — Salem, Mass.
Bunker, Lyman — Peabody, "
Bunker, Emily — Salem, "
Bunker, Sadie — Concord, "
Burns, O. E. — Yountrille, Cal.
Burleigh, Mrs. B. — Concord, N. H.
Burnham, Daniel — New Durham, N. H.
Buntin, Mrs. Wm. E — Woodstock, Conn.
Buzzell, Alfred — Barrington, N. H.
Bickford, A. H. — Boston, Mass.
Bickford, A. L. — Union Ridge Iowa.
Bickford, Moses — Northwood, N. H.
Blaisdell, Mrs. Bertie — Somersworth, "
Blaisdell, Mrs. Harriet — Elmwood, R. I.
Blanchard, John E. — Concord, N. H.
Blanchard, Mrs. S. M. — Hudson, "
Blanchard, Mrs. R. M. — Augusta, Ga.
*Blake, Dr. Jeremiah — Gilmanton, N. H.
*Blake, H. D. — Pittsfield, "

Blake, Mrs. Ella	Springfield, Mass.
Bodge, James	Fall River, "
Bodge, Ezra	" "
Bodge, Mrs. Fanny H.	Madbury, N. H.
Bowen, Mrs. Paulina	Concord, "
Brooks, Mrs. E. A.	Manchester, N. H.
Brewster, Mrs. E. V.	Dover, "
Brown, Geo. W.	" "
Brown, G. S.	Clarksville, "
Blunt, D. D.	Quincy, Cal.
Canfield, Rev. H.	Providence, R. I.
*Canney, Dr. H. C.	Manchester, N. H.
Canney, Rev. A. J.	Dakota.
Canney, John N.	Dover, N. H.
Carpenter, Mrs. E.	Ellenburg, N. Y.
Carr, Mrs. Laura Garland	Concord, N. H.
Carroll, Henry	Tamworth, "
Cate, John	Candia, "
Cate, Mrs. Abigail	East Flatbush, N. Y.
*Cate, N. E.	Northwood, N. H.
Caswell, M. G.	Pittsfield, "
Caswell, L. O.	Palatka, Fla.
Caswell, A. B.	Rumney, N. H.
Caswell, G. B.	Lynn, Mass.
Caswell, Edith	Canterbury, N. H.
Caswell, Mary H.	" "
Caswell, Nancy O.	" "
Caswell, George	Strafford "
Caswell, Charles	Philadelphia, Pa.
Caswell, Bartlett	" "
Chapman, Mrs S.	East Dennis, Mass.
Chamberlin, Mrs. H.	New Durham, N. H.
Chamberlin, Mrs. F. J.	Farmington, "
Chamberlin, Mrs. D. C. N.	Lawrence, Mass.
Chamberlin, S. C.	Albany, Vt.

THE BARNSTEAD REUNION.   111

*Chesley, Orrin F.	Dover, N. H.
Chesley, H. L.	" "
Chesley, Mrs. Jane	Concord, "
Chesley, Dr. C. C.	Dover, "
Chesley, Lyman	Frankfort, Kan.
Chates, Mrs. H. J.	Underhill, Vt.
Cilley, Wm. P.	Belmont, N. H.
*Cilley, Sewell J.	Rochester, "
Cilley, Mrs. S.	" "
*Cilley, George H.	Westfield, Iowa.
Cilley, Mrs. J. M.	Barrington, N. H.
Clough, John	Rochester, "
Clough, C. W.	Lynn, Mass.
Clough, Horace	Newmarket, N. H.
Clough, Frank W.	" "
Clough, Geo. H.	Rochester, "
Clough, Mrs. M.	Warrensburg, Ill.
Clough, Wm. A.	Concord, N. H.
*Collins, T. T.	Alton, "
Collins, John	" "
*Collins, C. F.	Pittsfield, "
Colbath, John	Farmington, N. H.
Couch, Mrs. John	Lawrence, Mass.
Clark, Judge L. W.	Manchester, N. H.
Clark, Mrs. Cora	Concord, N. H.
*Clark, Bradbury	Harristown, Ill.
Clark, Everett	Boston, Mass.
Clark, Alonzo	" "
Clark, Emma	Pittsfield, N. H.
Clark, George D.	Rochester, "
*Clark, Solomon	Pittsfield, "
Clark, Calvin D.	" "
*Clark, S. H.	Lynn, Mass.
Clark, Jos. W.	" "
Clark, Henry	" "
Clark, Frank	" "

Clark, John	Lynn, Mass.
Clark, Jewett	" "
Clark, J. P.	" "
Clark, Alvin	" "
Clark, Albert	Worcester, Mass.
*Clark, David	Albion, Neb.
Clark, Evalyn F.	Concord, N. H.
Clark, Frank H.	" "
Clark, Abram S.	Strafford, N. H.
Clark, Wm. B.	Sioux City, Iowa.
Clark, Frank	" "
*Clark, R. S.	Westfield, "
Clark, E. K.	Laconia, N. H.
Clark, Mrs. M. A.	Pittsfield, "
Clark, Jacob	Rochester, "
Clark, Almira	" "
Clark, Sydney	Somersworth, N. H.
Clark, Mrs. S. A.	" "
Clark, J. P.	Los Angelos, Cal.
Clark, Mrs. Alice G.	Pittsfield, N. H.
Copp, Frank	Newmarket,"
Copp, Mrs. Geo.	" "
Cole, Selathiel,	Pittsfield, "
Cole, Frank S.	" "
Cook, Mrs. Eva	Porter, Me.
Cook, Ira A.	Milton N. H.
Cox, Mrs. Nancy N.	Manchester, N. H.
Cooms, Mrs. M. J.	Ellensburg, N. Y.
Courser, Mrs. Abby H.	Henniker N. H.
Crockett, William	Boston, Mass.
*Crosby, John Q.	Farmington, N. H.
*Crosby, Eben	" "
Crosby, Sarah J.	" "
Currier, C. C.	Tilton, "
Dame, Miss Harriet P.	Washington, D. C.

THE BARNSTEAD REUNION. 113

Daniels, Harry P.   Nottingham, N. H.
Daniels, Ira   Somersworth, "
Daniels, Mrs. Enoch   " "
*Davis, D. F.   Bethlehem, "
Davis, Seth W.   Rochester, "
Davis, E. G.   Lee, "
Davis, George   Farmington, "
Davis, John   " "
Davis, Ira   Milton, "
Davis, Hiram   Laconia, "
Davis, S. P.   Alton, "
Davis, Mrs. Martha   Davenport, Iowa.
Davis, Smith, Jr.   Lynn, Mass.
*Davis, Horace   Pittsfield, N. H.
Davis, Ebenezer   St. Johnsbury Vt.
Davis, Nancy,   Pittsfield, N. H.
Davis, Frank   Haverhill, Mass.
*Davis, David B.   Pittsfield, N. H.
*Davis, Smith   Laconia, "
Davis, J. R. C.   Pittsfield, "
Davis, Mrs Betsey   Northwood, "
Davis, Charles B.   Whitefield, "
Day, Merven   Ludlow, Vt.
Daggett, Mrs. N. P   Rochester, N. H.
Daggett, Alpheus   Providence, R. I.
*Dennett, Geo. S.   Concord, N. H.
*Dennett, Charles   " "
*Dennett, Mark A.   Gilmanton, "
Dennett, Dr. John P.   Gloucester, Mass.
Dennett, Dr. H. E.   Boston, "
Demeritt, Mrs. Thomas   Northwood, N. H.
Demeritt, Mrs. Maria   Farmington, Maine.
Dean, Mrs. Nancy
Dearborn, Mrs. H.   New York City.
Dimond, Mrs. H.   Danville N. H.
Durgin, Frank G.   Pittsfield, "

Durgin, Helen — Pittsfield N. H.
Durgin, Mrs. Geo.   "   "
Durgin, Mrs. J. M. — Haverhill, Mass.
Dockham, Warren — Newburyport, Mass.
Dockham, Gowen   "   "
Dockham, Joseph   "   "
Dockham, George   "   "
Dorr, Prof. H. I. — Philadelphia, Pa.
Dorr, Etta W. — New York City.
Dore, Mrs. Herbert — Farmington, N. H.
Downs, George — Beverly, Mass.
Dodge, Mrs. H. A. — Concord, N. H.
Drake, Mrs. George — Pittsfield, "
Dow, Chas. J. — West Lebanon, N. H.
*Dow, John C. — Cambridgeport, Mass.
Dow, Fred.   "   "
Dow, William H.   "   "
Dow, Samuel — Campton, N. H.
*Drew, Aaron W. — Quincy, Cal.
Drew, Wm. Garland   "   "
Drew, Orrin G. — Newton, Iowa.
Drew, Alvin — Fremont, Ohio.
Drew, Obed — Newton, Iowa.
Drew, Geo. W. — Boston, Mass.
Drew, Cortes — Lawrence, Mass.
Drew, Horace — Gilmanton, N. H.
Drew, Mrs. Sally — Laconia, "
*Dudley, John H., — Farmington, "
*Dudley, Charles — E. Concord, "
Dudley, Charles V. — Brooklyn, N. Y.
*Dudley George W. — Concord, N. H.
Dudley, Mrs. Thomas — Gilmanton, "

Eaton, Mrs. D. F. — Pittsfield, "
Eaton, Rosie I.   "   "
Eaton, Mrs Abbie   "   "

Eaton, Mrs. John   Manchester, N. H.
Eaton, Dr. Lysander   St. Louis, Mo.
Eaton, Samuel P.   Strafford, N. H.
Eaton, William   Loudon,   "
Eastman, Mrs. Frank   Odgen, Kan.
Edgerly, Hon. M. V. B.   Manchester, N. H.
Edgerly, Prof. J. G.   Fitchburg, Mass.
Edgerly, A. J.   Manchester, N. H.
*Edgerly, D. G.   Gilmanton,   "
Edgerly, Isaiah   Wadley's Falls, N. H.
Edgerly, Mrs. E. G.   Pittsfield,   "
Edgerly, Amy L.   Haverhill, Mass.
Edgerly, Geo. E.   Pittsfield, N. H.
Edgerly, Cynthia A.   Gilmanton, "
Edgerly, Reuben   "   "
Edgerly, Laura   "   "
Edgerly, Horace   "   "
Edgerly, Mrs. David   Newburyport, Mass.
Edgerly, Mrs. E.   Pittsfield, N. H.
Elkins, Dr. J. P.   New London, N. H.
Elkins, Dr. J. S.   Farmington,   "
Elkins, Mrs. S. F.   "   "
Emery, Mrs. Mary A.   Boston, Mass.
*Emerson, Dr. James   Gardiner, Mass.
*Emerson, Jere E.   Pittsfield, N. H.
Emerson, Frank   "   "
Emerson, Mrs. Julia A.   Pittsfield,   "
Emerson, Luther   Westfield,   "
Emerson, Charles   Odgen, Kan.
Emerson, J. A.   "   "
*Emerson, A. J.   Pittsfield, N. H.
Emerson, John O.   Alton,   "
*Emerson, R. J.   Lynn, Mass.
Emerson, Bela   Effingham, N. H.
Emerson, Eliphalet   "   "
Emerson, Mrs. Julia   Farmington, "

Emerson, Mrs. Clara S.	Pittsfield, N. H.
*Evans, William	" "
Flanders, Mrs. Sally	Amesbury, Mass.
Flanders, Mrs. Charles	" "
*Flanders, Enoch	Alton, N. H.
Flanders, J. D.	" "
Fogg, C. W.	Lynn, Mass.
Fogg, Mrs. Lucy	" "
Forbes, Mrs. Hubbard	Sutton, Vt.
*Frost, Mrs. William	No. Andover Mass.
Foss, Mrs. Flora	Rochester, N. H.
Fuller, Mrs. George	Medford, Mass.
Furber, Mrs. Samuel	Alton, N. H.
Furber, Mrs. Mary A.	" "
*French, Charles S.	Pittsfield, N. H.
French, Mrs. Abram	" "
French, Mrs. Augusta	Loudon, "
French, Mrs. Mercy	Ipswich, Mass.
French, Rev. O. S.	Bangor, Me.
French, Lucian	So. Sangerfield, Me.
French, A. F.	Galveston, Texas.
French, C. W.	New York City.
French, J. C.	Concord, N. H.
French, Mrs. R. L.	Pittsfield N. H.
*French, Levi F.	Greeley, Col.
French, John P. H.	Farmington, N. H.
Garland, Dr. A. H.	" "
Garland, H. H.	Coleville, Kansas.
Garland, Frank	Chicago, Ill.
Garland, Frink	" "
Garland, Mrs. Mary D.	Kingston N. H.
Garland, Mrs. Betsey	Alton, "
Garland, Miss Josephine	" "
Garland, Charles H.	Sheffield, Vt.

Gear, Albert — Rochester, N. H.
Grandy, Mrs. H. A. — Concord, "
Grover, Mrs. Wm. — Exeter, "
George, Dr. Franklin — Macon, Georgia.
George, John A. — Portsmouth, N. H.
*George, Henry W. — Pittsfield, "
George, Frank O. — " "
Grace, Chas. S. — Haverhill, Mass.
Grace, Frank — " "
Gray, Woodbury — Beverly, Mass.
Gray, B. G. P. — " "
Gray, Orris D. — " "
Gray, Amos F. — Pittsfield, N. H.
Gray Mrs. Mary H. — Wheelock, Vt.
*Goodwin, Samuel E., — New York City.
Goodwin, Gilman — " "
*Godfrey, James — Lynn, Mass.
Griffin, Betsey — Lowell, Mass.
Griffin, Charles — " "
Greene, Wm. R. — Concord, Mass.
Greenwood, Sidney F. — Lynn, Mass.

Hall, J. Frank — Farmington, N. H.
*Hall, Stacy — " "
Hall, Oram R. — Dover, N. H.
Hall, Joseph D. — Stoneham, Mass.
*Hall, Burley — Rochester, N. H.
Hall, Mrs F. H. — Strafford, "
Hall, Joseph — " "
Hall, J. O. — Nottingham, N. H.
Hall, John S. — Concord, "
Hall, Mrs. Daniel — Strafford, "
Hall, Mrs. W. O. — Linden, Mass.
Hayes, Dr. Jos. R. — Lowell, "
Hayes, Geo. W. — Dover, N. H.
Hayes, Stephen — Worcester, Mass.

Hayes, Jesse — Holstein, Mass.
Hayes, Alvin — Cambridgeport, Mass.
Hayes, Orrin P. — Lynn, "
Hayes, W. W. — Farmington, N. H.
Hayes, Mrs. Lizzie — Lynn, Mass.
Hayes, Mrs. Sally T. — Dover, N. H.
Hayes, W. P. — " "
Hayes, John — Black Hills, Dakota.
Hayes, J. F. C. — Cleveland, Ohio.
Hayes, Eben — Gilmanton, N. H.
Hayes, Smith — Ipswich, Mass.
Hatch, Mrs. E. — Beverly, Mass.
Hanscame, John — Northwood, N. H.
Hanscame, Mrs Mary F. — " "
Hanscame, Julia — Boston, Mass.
*Hanscame, Lemuel — Epsom, N. H.
Hanscame, Jeremiah — Rochester, N. H.
*Hanscame, A. F. — Lynn, Mass.
Hanscame, Ada — Strafford, N. H.
Hanson, John, — Salem, Ohio.
Hanson, Luther N. — Cyhoga Falls, Ohio.
Hanson, George — Perrysburg, "
Hanson, Dr. C. W. — Northwood, N. H.
Hanson, Lewis — Washington, D. C.
Hanson, Jos. B. — Taunton, Mass.
Harvey, Rev. Jos. — Pittsfield, N. H.
Hawkins, Ella S. — Ellenburg, N. Y.
Hadley Mrs Eva E. — Concord, N. H.
Higgins, Mrs. F. S. — Manchester, N H.
Herring, Mrs. James — Farmington, "
*Hoitt, Col. James S. — Laconia, "
*Hoitt, John S. — Concord, "
Hoitt, John G. — " "
*Howard, J. W. — Alton, "
*Howard, Hanson — Strafford, "
Howard, William — Boston, Mass.

Hooper, Mrs. William — Dover, N. H.
Hooper, Mrs. Delia — Berwick, Maine.
Horne, James — Acton, "
Horne, Mrs. Mary A. — Farmington, N. H.
Hussey, Mrs. B. — Gilmanton, "
Hurd, Albert — Pittsfield, "
*Ham, Dr. O. F. — Bethlehem, "
Ham, Mrs. John — Mishewakie, Indiana.
Ham, Wm. F. — New York City.
*Ham, J. C. — Gilmanton, N. H.
Ham, Mrs. S. A. — Boston, Mass.
Ham, Ellen A. — Strafford, N. H.
Ham, Mrs. D. — Rochester, "
Ham, Mrs. Samuel — " "
Heath, Mrs. Lizzie — Gilmanton, "
Harmon, Mrs. M. E. — New Durham, N. H.
Holmes, Rev. D. G. — Chicago, Ill.
Holmes, Woodbury — Farmington, N. H.
Holmes, Mrs. Mary A. — Strafford, "
Holmes Mrs. Lydia — " "
Holmes, Charles A. — Middleton, Conn.
Holmes, Clara E. — " "
Holmes, Mary E. — Dover, N. H.
Holmes, Cora J. — Strafford, "
Homes, Mrs. Ellen — " "
Huse, Hon. H. H, — Manchester, N. H.
Huntress, Frank — Wolfeborough, "
Huntress, Nellie — Lynn, Mass.
Hackett, Mrs. Jere. — New Britain, Conn.
Hill, Ruel, — East Kingston, N. H.
Hill, Mrs. Mary — Northwood, "
Hill Wm. M. — E. Bowdoinham, Me.
Hill, Mrs. James R. — Concord, N. H.
Hill, Samuel — Northwood, "
*Hill, Warren B. — Pittsfield, "
Hill, Lewis A. — Alton, "

*Hill, Alexis A.	Lynn, Mass
Hill, Herbert M.	" "
Hill, Mrs. John	Pittsfield, N. H.
Hill, John D.	" "
Hill, Martha B.	Newmarket,"
Hill, Mrs. Samuel	Strafford, "
Hill, Jeremiah	Dunbar, Mich.
Hill, Benjamin	Laconia, N. H.
Hill, John S.	Saco, Me.
Hill, John H.	Amador, Cal.
Hill, Mrs. Jennie H.	Strafford, N. H.
Hill, John	Rochester, "
Hill, George	Manchester, "
*Hodgdon, S. A.	Chester, Iowa.
Hodgdon, Albert	Grinnell, "
Hodgdon, Charles	" "
Hodgdon, A. E.	" "
Hodgdon, Frank L.	Davenport, Iowa.
Hodgdon, G. W.	Gilmanton, N. H.
Hodgdon, Lyman	Dover, "
Hodgdon, Wm. A.	St. Louis, Mo.
*Hobbs, George	Pittsfield N. H.
Hobbs, Frank	Lynn, Mass.
Hobbs, Mrs. M.	Davenport, Iowa.
Jewett, Rev. S. D.	Middletown, Conn.
Jacobs, T. S.	Manchester, N. H.
Jacoby, Mrs. S. F.	Wilton, Iowa.
Jenkins, C. E.	Pittsfield, N. H.
Jenkins, Miss Sadie	Porter, Me.
*Jenkins, William	West Plattsburg, N. Y.
Jenkins, Louisa	Boston, Mass.
Jenkins, Mary H.	" "
Jenkins, Orrin J.	Pittsfield, N. H.
*Jenkins, Lewis	Gilmanton, "
Jenkins, Melvin J.	Manchester, "

THE BARNSTEAD REUNION. 121

Jenkins, Jos. J.	Effingham, N. H. .
Jenkins, James	Concord, "
Jenkins, Jethro	" "
Johnson, Mrs. John	No. Berwick, Me.
Johnson, Augustus	Live Oaks, Florida.
Joy, Albert H.	Pittsfield, N. H.
Joy, Charles	Durham, "
Joy, Annie	Worcester, Mass.
*Jones, George H.	Sanborn, Iowa.
Jones, Jenny L.	Dover, N. H.
Jones, Mrs. William	Pittsfield, "
Jenness, Mrs. J. J.	" "
Jenness, Mrs. Sarah	Rochester, "
Jenness, Susan	" "
Kent, Hon. J. Horace	Portsmouth, N. H.
*Kaime, James	Canterbury, "
Kaime, Joanna	" "
Kaime, G. W.	Warrensburg, Ill.
Kaime, Kingsbury G.	No. Woburn, Mass.
Kaime, Samuel J.	Stoneham, "
Kaime, Mrs. Belle	St. Louis, Mo.
Kaime, George	Oshkosh, Wis.
Keniston, George	Wolfeborough, N. H.
*Keniston, Eben	Somersworth, "
Keniston, G. W.	" "
Killem, Mrs. M. A.	Lawrence, Kan.
Kimball, Mrs. J. W. M.	Alton, N. H.
Knowlton, Mrs. L. A.	Pittsfield, "
Knox, Nettie,	Pembroke, "
*Knowles, G. F.	Lynn, Mass.
Knowles, S. P.	" "
Lang, Mrs. J. J.	Alton, N. H.
Lang, Mrs. M. V. B.	Farmington, "
Labaron, J. D.	Cambridge, Mass.

*Langley, Joseph T.   Pittsfield, N. H.
Langley, Wm. N.   Exeter,   "
Lee, Augustus   Rochester,   "
Lee, Mrs. Daniel   Barrington,   "
Lodge, Mrs. L.   Neola, Iowa.
Lougee, Simeon   Farmington, N. H.
Lougee, Mrs. Dr.   Rochester,   "
Leighton, Susie P.   Farmington,   "
Lord, John   Manchester,   "
*Lord, Horace   Salem, Mass.
Locke, Mrs. James   Farmington, N. H.
Longfellow, Mrs. M. S.   Groveland, Mass.
Loud, Mrs. A.   Portsmouth N. H.
Littlefield, Lavina   Kennebunk, Me.
Littlefield, W. P.   Rollinsford, N. H.
Littlefield, David   Dover,   "
Littlefield, Mrs. Susan   New Durham,   "
Lyford, F. H. Rev.   Littleton,   "

Marston, Nettie   Chichester,   "
Mason, Mrs. Hannah   Canterbury,   "
Marden, Mrs. D. H.   Chichester,   "
Mayo, Mrs. J. F.   Boston, Mass.
*McNeal, John,   Chicago, Ill.
McNeal, D. W.   "   "
McFarland, Mrs. Wm.   Concord, N. H.
McNeil, William   Haverhill, Mass.
McDuffee, Mrs Jane   Tewksbury,   "
*Meader, J. G.   Boscawen, N. H.
Meader, Mrs. D. P.   Newmarket,   "
Marble, George   Somersworth, "
Marsh, D. K.   Concord,   "
Marsh, Hiram   "   "
Murphy, Hon. C. M.   Dover,   "
Munsey, Dr. Geo. Frank   Greenville,   "
*Munsey, Curtis C.   Danvers, Mass.

*Munsey, Woodbury	Pittsfield, N. H.
Munsey, Robert	Chichester, "
Munsey, G. W.	Gilmanton, "
Munsey, D. C.	Lampasas, Texas.
Munsey, Mrs. Mahala	Dover, N. H.
Munsey, Georgia	" "
Munsey, A. T.	Colorado.
Munsey, H. W.	Lynn, Mass.
Munsey, Frank L.	Goffs Falls, N. H.
Munsey, Levi D.	Clarksville, "
*Murray, James	Middletown, Ill.
Murray, Mrs. Nancy	St. Paul, Minn.
Marshall, Andrew	Pittsfield, N. H.
*Merrill, J. B.	Concord, "
Merrill, S. F.	Euclair, Wis.
Merrill, Frank	New York City.
Merrill, Lyman	Concord, N. H.
Merrill, Mrs. Sarah	Gilmanton, "
Merrill, Mrs. Maria	Pittsfield "
Merrill, C. E.	Gilmanton, "
Merrill, Dr. S. A.	Belmont, "
Miles, Sarah A.	Sheffield, Vt.
Miller, Mrs. Eliphalet	Lowell, Mass.
Miller, Mrs. Harry	Concord, N. H.
*Morrison, Abram	Madbury, "
Morrison, John	So. Berwick, Me.
Morrison, Mrs. D. H.	Alton, N. H.
Morrison, Mrs. J. I. N.	" "
Morrison, G. W.	" "
Morrison, Mrs. Sarah	Boston, Mass.
*Mooney, H. P.	Pittsfield, "
Morrill, Rev. James	Pittsfield, N. H.
Morrill, Mrs. H.	" "
Morrill, Jos. G.	" "
Morrill, Josephine	" "
Morrill, Mrs. C.	" "

Moore, Mrs. L. F.   Manchester, N. H.

Newell, Hon. J. P.   "   "
Newell, Wm. H.   Gilmanton,   "
Newell, Albert H.   "   "
*Newell, Moses D,   Elo, Wis.
Newell, Chas. D.   Albion, Neb.
*Newell, Wm, J.   St. Joe, Hamilton Co.,
Newell, Samuel A.   York Co., Neb. [Neb.
Newell, L. V.   Portsmouth, N. H.
Newell, Dr. A. C.   Albion, Neb.
Nelson, Edward   Gilmanton N. H.
Noyes, Mrs. G. F. A.   Lynn, Mass.
Nutter, Col. E. S.   Concord, N. H.
Nutter, James,   Worcester, Mass.
Nutter, Hon. John D.   Montreal, Canada.
Nutter, Benjamin   Toronto, Canada.
Nutter, Geo. L.   Lynn, Mass.
*Nutter, James, 2d,   Bear Grove, Minn.
Nutter, Van D.   Northwood, N. H.
Nutter, John   Pittsfield, "
*Nutter, Jas. A.   Swampscott, Mass.
Nutter, Joseph S.   Salem,   "
Nutter, William E.   Boston,   "
Nutter, John P.   Concord, N. H.
Nutter, Wm.   Gilmanton,   "
*Nutter, A. L.   Lynn, Mass.
*Nutter, Orrin S.   "   "
Nutter, C. W.   Rochester, N. H.
Nutter, Mercy   Gilmanton,   "
Nutter, Asa N.   Alton,   "
Nutter, Geo. E.   Dover,   "
Nutter, John M.   "   "
Nutter, Charles C.   Concord,   "
Nutter, Dr. G. W.   Manchester, "
Nutter, Franklin C.   Pittsfield, "

Nutter, David R.   Hopkinton, N. H.
Nutter, Ebenezer   Lynn, Mass.
Nutter, Nathan   Rochester, N. H.
Nutter, Chas. E.   Farmington, "
Nutter, George F.   Cedar Keys, Florida.
Nutter, J. H.   Somersworth, N. H.
Nutter, John C.   Rochester, "
Nutter, Mrs. G. L.   Concord, "

*Otis, Joseph   Newmarket, "
Otis, Mrs. Ai   Farmington, "
Otis, Mrs. Sarah   Strafford, "
Ordway, Louisa   Loudon, "
Osgood, Mrs. Perley   " "
Osgood, Dyer   " "

Parshley, Albert J.   Rochester, "
Parshley, J. J.   Vershire, Vt.
*Parshley, Ira   Pittsfield, N. H.
Parshley, John   " "
Palmer, Mrs. Hannah   Deerfield, "
Parker, Lavina   Epsom, "
Parmenter, Nellie   Farmington, "
*Page, Winthrop   Pittsfield, "
Page, Hiram   " "
Page, Nathaniel   Gilmanton, "
Patterson, Mrs. Helen   Lynn, Mass.
Parsons, Rufus   Gilmanton, N. H.
Pettigrew, Frank   Newmarket, "
Pettigrew, Mary J.   " "
Perry, Mrs. H. J.   Manchester, "
Perry, James   Lynn, Mass.
Pendergast, Hon. Geo. S.   Boston, Mass.
*Pendergast, Isaac S.   Newmarket, N. H.
Pendergast, Nancy   Boston, Mass.
*Pendergast, Charles F.   Newmarket, N. H.

Pendergast, John H.	Salisbury, Mass.
Pendergast, Jas. A.	Saux Centre, Minn.
Pendergast, Solomon	" "
*Pendergast, George E.	Cleveland, Ohio.
Pendergast, John B.	Chicago, Ill.
Pendergast, Mrs A. M.	Lynn, Mass.
Pendergast, Jane	Alton, N. H.
Pendergast, Frank C.	Concord, "
Perkins, True	Pittsfield, "
Perkins, Mrs. John	Loudon, "
Perkins, Mrs. Charles	Concord, "
Perkins, Mrs. Samuel	Pittsfield, "
Prescott, Mrs. Perley	Farmington, N. H.
Prescott, Mrs. Miranda	Hampton Falls, N. H.
Pray, Mattie A.	Dover, "
Proctor, William	Haverhill, Mass.
Proctor, Samuel N.	Lowell, "
*Proctor, Thomas D.	Beverly, "
*Pickering, Hon. J. L.	Concord, N. H.
Pickering, Mark	Cambridgeport, Mass.
Pickering, Joseph	Salem, Mass.
*Pickering, C. C.	Newport, Me.
Pickering, Nathan	Durham, N. H.
Pickering, Calvin	" "
Pickering, Fred.	Concord, "
Pickering, Mrs. John	Boston, Mass.
Pierce, Henry H.	Pittsfield, N. H.
*Pierce, Albert	Lynn, Mass.
Pitman, Dr. Eben	Boston, "
Pitman, A. J.	" "
Pitman, Samuel	Strafford, N. H.
Pitman, Joseph	" "
Pitman, Mrs. Jona.	Manchester, "
Pitman, Alvin	Lynn, Mass.
*Pitman, C. H.	Farmington, N. H.
Pitman, Frank D.	" "

Pitman, John T.	Pelham, N. H.
Pitman N. T.	Concord, "
Pitman, Mrs. Emma	Farmington, "
Pitman, John	Alexandria "
Pitman, George	Danvers, Mass.
Pitman, Lougee	Manistee, Mich.
Pitman, Eben, Jr.	Bath, Me.
Pitman, Susan	Lowell, Mass.
Pitman, R. M.	" "
Piper, Rev. C. E.	Wakefield, Mass.
Piper, Mrs. Mary E.	Gilmanton, N. H.
Quint, Alonzo Hall, D. D.	Dover, "
Quimby, Rev. M. A.	Gilmanton, "
Rand, Dr. Jos. B.	Hartford, Vt.
Rand, Elizabeth	Lowell, Mass.
Rand, Chas. F.	Alton, N. H.
Randall, Mrs. Belle	So. Brooks, Me.
Randall, Mrs. A. S.	Pittsfield, N. H.
*Randall, Jeremiah	Gilmanton, N. H.
Randlett, Mrs. J. F.	Boston, Mass.
Ricker, Joseph	Portland, Me.
Riddler, Mrs. Nancy E.	Boston, Mass.
Rines, Mrs. Emily	Concord, N. H.
Russ, Mrs. Hattie A.	Ossipee, "
Russell, Jos. C.	Boston, Mass.
Rollins, Samuel G.	E. Boston, "
Rollins, John M.	Oshkosh, Wis.
Rollins, T. E.	Corning, N. Y.
Rollins, Mrs. J. W.	Boston, Mass.
Rollins, Mrs. A. L.	Alton, N. H.
*Roberts, Geo. S.	Warrensburg, Ill.
Roberts, Jona. E.	" "
Roberts, Frank	" "
Robinson, Mrs. Phebe	Dover, N. H.

Ross, John	Salem, Mass.
Sinclair, Hon. John G.	Florida.
Savage, Mrs. Moses H.	Boston, Mass.
*Sackett, Hiram M.	Pittsfield, N. H.
Sackett, Frank E.	Lynn, Mass.
Sargent, John	Boston, "
Sargent, Mrs. Harriet	Hopkinton, N. H.
Sanborn, Mrs. Mary	So. Newmarket, N. H.
Sanborn, Dr. G. H.	Henniker, "
Sanders, Mrs. W. C.	Greeley, Colorado.
Selden, Mrs. John	Pittsfield, N. H.
Scruton, Thomas	Strafford, "
Scruton, Walter G.	Pittsfield, "
Scribner, Mrs. S.	Lewiston, Me.
Scriggins, Joshua C.	Storm Lake, Iowa.
Scriggins, Charles	Sandwich, N. H.
Scriggins, William	" "
Seward, G. H.	Alton, "
*Seward, Frank	" "
Smith, Mrs. Josephine	Concord, "
Smith, Geo. F.	" "
Smith, George	Campton, "
Smith, Mrs. C.	Centre Harbor, N. H.
Small, Alden	Strafford, "
*Smart, N. T.	Effingham, "
*Smart, Ansil C.	Concord, "
Smart, F. A. J.	Effingham, "
Smart, Mrs. Mary	Washington, D. C.
Simpson, Mrs. S. A.	Lynn, Mass.
Snell, George,	Pittsfield, N. H.
Snell, Clement	" "
Snell, Darius	Pembroke, "
Sleeper, J. O.	Rochester, "
Sleeper, C. W.	" "
Sleeper, Mrs. B. F.	Farmington, "

Souza, Mrs. A. J.   Concord, N. H.
Spencer, Alvin   Somersworth, "
Shepard, Luther E.   Lowell, Mass.
*Shackford, William   Concord, N. H.
Shackford, James   "   "
*Shackford, H. H.   Saugus, Mass.
*Shackford, A. W.   Farmington, N. H.
Shackford, Alphonso   Providence, R. I.
Shackford, Elbridge G.   Dubuque, Iowa.
Shackford, Charles J.   Lynn, Mass.
Shannon, Nathaniel H.   Rochester, N. H.
Shaw, Mrs. Emily   Pittsfield, "
Short, Mrs. Abbie E.   Boston, Mass.
Standish, Mrs. L. Miles   "   "
Stanton, Mark   Barrington, N. H.
*Straw, Samuel   Concord, "
Straw, John W.   "   "
Straw, Edwin D.   Farmington, "
Straw, Alonzo   "   "
Straw, Simon   Alton, "

*Tasker, J. M.   Myrtle St., Lynn, Mass.
Tasker, Frank   "   "   "
Tasker, Mrs. Seth   Boston, "
Tasker, Mrs. Gilbert   Strafford, N. H.
Tasker, Mrs. Joseph   Pittsfield, "
Tasker, Mary   Boston, Mass.
Tebbetts, Orran W., Esq.   Laconia, N. H.
*Tebbetts, Israel C.   "   "
Tebbetts, Daniel P.   Manchester, N. H.
Tebbetts, Ephraim   Salem, Mass.
Tebbetts, Mrs. Ella   Lynn, "
Tebbetts, Mrs. Addie,   Franklin, N. H.
Tuttle, Hon. H. A.   Pittsfield, "
Tuttle, Judge John   Farmington, "
*Tuttle, Henry F.   Pittsfield, "

Tuttle, Chas. S.	Nashua, N. H.
Tuttle, Frank P.	" "
Tuttle, Mrs. George	Pittsfield, "
Tutttle, Mrs. C. H.	Augusta, Georgia.
Tuttle, Mrs. Albert G.	New York City.
Thompson, Mrs. A. H.	St. Stephens, N. B.
*Thompson, Edward	So. Berwick, Me.
Thompson, Edward, Jr.	" "
Thompson, William	" "
Towle, Hon. Geo. H.	Deerfield, N. H.
Towle, Roby M.	" "
Towle, Frank	Northwood, "
Towle, Samuel	" "
Towle, Daniel	" "
Towle, James	Haverhill, Mass.
Towle, Mrs. Betsey	Pittfield, N. H.
Towle, Mrs. Susan	Kingston, "
Twombly, Mrs. Elvira	Strafford, "
Twombly, Mrs. Emily	Pittsfield, "
Walker, Dr. A. C.	Greenfield, Mass.
Walker, George F.	Newmarket, N. H.
Walker, Mrs. R. D. K.	Portsmouth, "
Walker, Ansel G.	Detroit, Mich.
Walker, Samuel	Newmarket, N. H.
Walker, Mrs. Hannah	Gilmanton, "
Walker, Miss Sarah E.	Dover, "
Wallace, Mrs. James	Charlestown, Mass.
Wallace, Mrs. Wm.	Northwood, N. H.
*Waldron, Oliver	Madbury, N. H.
Warren, Dr. Albert	Madrid, Spain.
Watkins, Mrs. Geo.	Portsmouth, N. H.
Watson, Mrs. J.	Gilmanton, "
*Webster, Hon. R. S.	Melrose, Mass.
Welch, Eben	Lowell, "
Welch, Samuel	Boston, "

Welch, Clark	Strafford, N. H.
Welch, Edwin	Rochester, "
Welch, Mrs. Mary	Battle Creek, Mich.
Welch, Timothy	Pittsfield, N. H.
Welch, Frank	Strafford, "
*Wheeler, Dr. John	Pittsfield, "
Wheeler, Dr. P. H.	Alton, "
*Wheeler, Luke	Westfield, Iowa.
Whitcomb, D. H.	Fitzwilliam, N. H.
Whittier, Mrs. H.	Portsmouth, "
White, Rev. F. J.	Chester, "
*Wentworth, Henry R.	Dover, "
*Wentworth, A. J.	New Durham, "
*Wentworth, C. W.	Lynn, Mass.
Winkley, Alonzo	Lawrence, "
Winkley, J. M.	Stoneham, "
Winkley, Mrs. J. O.	Chelsea, "
Winkley, Benjamin	Strafford, N. H.
Winkley, David	Berwick, Me.
Winkley, W. P.	Chicopee, Mass.
*Winkley, John S.	Strafford, N. H.
Winkley, Mrs. D. B.	" "
Winkley, Paul H.	" "
Wingate, William	Farmington, "
Wingate, Mrs. Lyman	Rochester, "
Willey, Everett	Lynn, Mass.
Willard, Richard	Sutton, Vt.
Willard, Mrs. John	" "
Willard, Oliver	Barton, "
Woodward, William	Exeter, N. H.
Woodward, Edwin	" "
*Woodhouse, J. L.	Walnut, Iowa.
Woodhouse, John L.	Wilton, "
Woodhouse, Mrs. G. W.	Laconia, N. H.
Woodhouse, Dr. N. W.	Wilton, Iowa.

Young, Dr. S. W.   Pittsfield, N. H.
Young, Dr. Lysander   Candia,   "
Young, Mrs. Salma L.   Lynn, Mass.
*Young, Stephen   "   "
Young, A. J.   Pittsfield, N. H.
Young, G. W.   Laconia, N. H.
Young, A. W.   Lynn, Mass.
Young, H. A.   "   "
Young, Alva A.   Concord, N. H.
Young, George   Ipswich, Mass.
York, Mrs. R. G.   Farmington, N. H.

www.ingramcontent.com/pod-product-compliance
Lightning Source LLC
Chambersburg PA
CBHW030340170426
43202CB00010B/1187